Books by Glenn Andrews

MOOD FOOD (1974)

IMPROMPTU COOKING (1973)

MOOD FOOD

MOOD FOOD

Glenn Andrews

ATHENEUM

New York

1974

To happy memories of my wonderful mother and grandmother, GLENN HUNTER ELLIS *and* ELIZABETH HUNTER STERNBERG—*and with thanks to* HOPE PEEK *for her talents as friend and indexer, and to* MARIANNE CASEY *and my daughter* KATIE DOHERTY *for their great and kindly help in the preparation of the manuscript.*

INTRODUCTION

WHAT IS MOOD FOOD? It's food—and drink—to help you cope with or control all sorts of bad moods: to soothe you, calm you, comfort you, warm you, cool you, sustain you, cheer you up, and generally make you feel better.

I told a friend I was writing a book about soothing, mood-changing food. "You know," I said, "food for when you're tired or discouraged and just need encouraging or bolstering-up. Her face grew dreamy. "Mmmmmmmm . . . mashed potatoes," she crooned. I've learned since then that almost everyone will give just such a quick and heartfelt response, and they all tell about their own favorite mood-improving foods with the same blissful fervor. They may never have thought about it before, but they all have a special food or foods to see them through their times of trial.

Few responses have been alike. "Eggnog," my son said immediately (and went off to fix one for himself). "Yogurt," someone else answered. "I want yogurt when I just don't want *any-*

thing else." That same person pointed out to me that soothing foods tend to be those you don't have to chew.

And she's right—things that just sort of slip down without much effort on your part are indeed soothing. As I began to make lists of the kinds of food that make you able to carry-on-no-matter-what, it became evident that a high proportion of them had this quality. Or if you do have to chew some of them a little, at least the pieces are rather small—bitesize—or very soft. Most of the time. Sometimes *crunch* is what you crave. It's all very individual.

What are some of the other qualities that make food help you conquer any sort of malaise? I think simplicity is the main thing. The foods that soothe are mostly basic, down-home dishes. Very little wine, few herbs. "Just the way it comes out of the ground," as my husband says. Or almost. Nothing to make any very great demands on you in the way of either preparation or appreciation. (Some of the dishes do take a little time to cook, though, so it's a good idea to keep them on hand in the freezer for any sort of physical, emotional or mental emergency.) There's one exception to this rule of simplicity: the elegant creations such as Chicken Poached in Lemon Juice that do the most for you when you're feeling a little seedy or run down at the heels. There are a number of these.

Dairy products turn up in many of the soothing foods, and so do vegetables, though not of the stock green beans *amandine* or *petit pois à la française* type. They're more apt to be puréed or at least slightly mashed, and they tend to swim in butter and cream; if there's a sauce, it's a simple, salubrious one. Practically all soups are soothing, and most desserts. The desserts also give you sugar's quick kick of energy. (Didn't Charles Lindbergh fly across the Atlantic sustained solely by chocolate bars? I think so, and I think this led a whole generation to turn to chocolate for strength.) There's meat in the soothing-food range, too, but it doesn't often play a star role—though there are times when nothing will do but a steak or a lamb or pork chop.

There's a theory, well-regarded in some circles, that what we crave to eat is what we need, that our bodies are smarter about these things than our minds. Maybe. It certainly makes a handy excuse, at any rate, for indulging ourselves in what sounds good at the moment. I do it all the time.

Another way of looking at this might be that the food we yearn for when we're depressed is the food our ancestors ate, cooked in their ways (which means primarily just thrown into a pot and boiled a while). That when we're so weary or discouraged that our veneer of "civilization" wears thin, we atavistically go back to the "old ways." I rather like this idea, but my anthropologist daughter would be the one to pursue it further. And I do know that some of the foods that suit various moods are strictly modern. No cave man ever sat down to a plateful of fried salt pork with cream gravy.

Some students of mankind might look at the preponderance of milk products and see a return to infancy, to the suckling babe. I don't know . . . that may be part of it. All I do know is that milk and cream and butter do nice things for me. (Just for my psyche, not for my figure.)

Don't think, however, that bland foods are the only ones that soothe. On a cold day, when half your problem is that you're half frozen, perhaps what you need is some chili to warm your soles and soul. Or when it's hot and you're utterly limp, *gazpacho* could be just the thing to make everything better, even though it's about the zippiest soup there is. In certain moments of tiredness, I put quite a lot of hot sauce into some cream, then bake cheese-sprinkled eggs on top of it (see page 82) and feel that it does quite a bit for me. It just depends—on you and on what particular combination of factors has you down.

❖ ❖ ❖

The mood-changing foods in this book are meant, in I think every case, to make up an entire meal. Even the desserts. (Pure bliss for me would be a huge bowl of chocolate bread pudding with hard sauce—with all guilt thoughts about the lack of vegetables and protein steadfastly shut down.) They are, however, most of them, good dishes to put into a complete menu, too. A purée of green beans in cream, for example (page 102), makes a gorgeously soothing meal, but it can also function as a glamorous vegetable for a dinner party.

In general, though, you'll make your meals of these foods a private matter. Sometimes an entire family or other group will be in need of restorative or calming food (say, after a long trip in a car), and the kindest deed possible would be to serve them all what they need. In my own family, after we've had a long day of one sort or another, someone will say, "Let's just have . . ." and everyone will smile and sigh softly. Or moan in agreement. It's usually baked eggs (page 82) that's requested, or Lobscouse, a very simple beef stew (see page 39), but my husband will put in an occasional bid for a cheese sandwich or say, "Why don't you just not serve *anything* for dinner tonight?" which means he wants to make himself an eggnog (page 229). Usually, though, it's just you, with your shoes off.

Even though most people do have their own special soothing foods—the ones they've found through the years and stuck with —there's a universality about these dishes, so that what works for someone else is very apt to work for you, too. Perhaps someone else's specialty for these occasions will work even better for you than your own. The problem is that when you're tired, discouraged, half-sick, etc., you're in no shape to be creative. You just fall back on the old standbys. Hence this book: a collection of the foods that have brought solace and strength to others. Give them a try.

In addition to a regular food index, there is a special *mood* index, beginning on page 241—practically everything that goes wrong should come under one of these headings or another. When you're limp from the heat. . . . When you're too tired to eat. . . . When a little elegance would help . . . and so on.

All the recipes, unless otherwise indicated, will feed one person in desperate need of succor or, in most cases, two or three more normal people. To feed more, just multiply the ingredients. Some of the listings, as you will see, are not recipes at all, but simply suggestions. For instance, my older daughter insists that ginger ale be included, and I'm certainly not going to give you a recipe for *that*.

CONTENTS

MOOD FOOD

SOUPS

WHAT CAN WARM YOU UP when the weather's cold, cool you off on a hot day—calm your nerves, no matter what? Give you strength when you need it, too, and act as a general panacea for your moods?

You guessed.

One or another of these soups should take care of just any sort of emotional crisis you might encounter. There's even a fruit soup in case a time arises when you want a soup but somehow feel a yen for something sweet, too. Soup's a cure-all. . . . Just try it and see.

Lentil Soup

I was at a friend's house one day recently when her husband arrived home from work. There had been a tumultuous rainstorm that afternoon, and though he had left his office early, he had hit such limited visibility, flooding and traffic jams that it took him two or three times longer than usual to get home. He was a wreck. "What are we having for dinner?" he asked. Proudly and happily his wife replied, *"Steak au poivre."* "Oh," he said, and looked even more destroyed. "I was hoping that maybe it could be lentil soup. My mother used to make lentil soup. . . ." About then I left, feeling sympathy for both of them.

A week or so later, the wife called me. "I'm making lentil soup," she said, "and it just doesn't seem to taste right. What can I add to it?" (People do things like this to you when you write cookbooks.) I gave her a suggestion or two; then she called again to say it *still* didn't taste right. And so on, for another call or two. I never heard if her husband was happy about his lentil soup. Probably that particular night he would have preferred *steak au poivre.*

Here's a good lentil soup. You won't have to call anyone to ask what to add to it (though if you have a ham bone and add it at the beginning of the cooking, the soup will be even better).

1 cup lentils, washed but not soaked

1 quart beef stock—homemade, canned or even made from good bouillon cubes

1 large stalk celery with leaves, minced

1 medium onion, minced

1 carrot, thinly sliced

A dash of powdered cloves (optional)

½ teaspoon salt (more later if needed)

A little black pepper

1 bay leaf

¼ teaspoon sugar

Juice of ½ lemon or ½ cup heavy cream

2 tablespoons butter

Croutons or hot-dog slices or sour cream or lemon slices or chopped parsley for garnish

Put everything except the lemon juice or heavy cream, butter and, of course, the garnish in a big pot. Simmer until the vegetables are tender—1 to 3 hours, depending on how small the pieces are and how low the fire under the pot. Blend or put through a food mill. Add the lemon juice or heavy cream and correct the seasoning (taste to see if it needs more salt and pepper). Stir in the butter.

Reheat to just below the boiling point. Serve garnished with croutons or hot-dog slices or a large dab of sour cream or a slice of lemon or just some chopped parsley.

Makes about 4 to 5 cups.

This freezes nicely, so you can have it all ready to thaw and heat any time you or someone you cook for has trouble, whether with a rainstorm or anything else.

Pozole

Pozole, a soup, is a Mexican hangover cure. What more do you need to know? If it can undo the ravages of too much tequila, it has to have eminently soothing qualities. Residents of *New* Mexico spell it *posole,* make many variations of it and don't seem to recommend it for hangovers. Perhaps they don't drink that much tequila.

This version is strictly my own. The real thing calls for pig's head, something I find in rather short supply in my neighborhood markets—even if I wanted to find it, I doubt if I could. (And even to see one would probably put most people into a state of shock.) Also, I use a jar of pickled pig's feet instead of the plain, straight-from-the-animal ones used in Mexico; this adds an unorthodox taste of vinegar, but I like that. I've made other changes, too, but still feel this is close enough to the original to be called *pozole.*

1 small jar pickled pig's feet
½ pound boneless pork, cut into small pieces
2 chicken wings
1 quart chicken broth
1 small onion, chopped
2 teaspoons chili powder
1 clove garlic, run through a press (or a little garlic salt or powder)
½ teaspoon oregano
Salt and pepper
½ cup canned hominy or kernel corn
Minced scallions, shredded lettuce, and thinly sliced radishes for garnish

Remove any bones from pig's feet. Combine them with the chicken wings, chicken broth, onion, chili powder, garlic, oregano, salt and pepper in a big pot. Simmer, covered, for 45 minutes. Then put the hominy, if you're able to find it, or the corn, into a blender container and whir it just for a moment. Add to the soup and simmer for 2 or 3 minutes more. Just before serving, stir in the scallions, lettuce and radishes. If you'd like the soup hotter, add a little more chili powder (mix it first with a small amount of the broth) or some red pepper flakes or chili pequins, which you'll find in the Spice Islands line.

Makes about 4 to 5 cups.

There's another standard Mexican hangover cure you might want to try: *menudo*. It's similar to *pozole*, but features tripe instead of pork and chicken, contains no chili powder and is not usually garnished with greenery.

Don't wait until you have a hangover before you try either *pozole* or *menudo*. (In fact, try not to have a hangover, ever.)

Split Pea Soup

Years ago, I read in some magazine that there is a custom in Holland of serving a very special soup on Christmas Eve. *Erwentsoep,* I believe it was called. Since it's fun to follow various holiday traditions—and since soup sounded like a good solution to the Christmas Eve frenzies—I tore out the clipping. Then, on December 23, I looked more closely at the instructions and discovered that *erwentsoep* was just my old friend split pea soup. *Everybody's* old friend split pea soup. It's soothing on Christmas Eve, yes, but also on 364 other days of the year.

1 cup green split peas
1 ham bone or 3 or 4 slices of bacon
2 quarts water (or use beef stock if you don't have a ham bone)
1 carrot, peeled and thinly sliced
1 onion, peeled and impaled with 2 cloves
½ bay leaf
Cream and/or butter (optional)
Croutons or thin slices of cooked hot dog for garnish

Combine split peas, ham bone or bacon, water, carrot, onion with cloves and bay leaf in a big soup pot. Simmer, covered, for an hour; then remove the bay leaf and cloves. You'll have a pretty good soup now, if you purée it. But for a better soup, simmer for an hour or two more, until everything but the ham bone is falling apart. Remove the ham bone. (There may still be visible pieces of carrot and onion. If so, and if you don't like the looks of them, purée even at this point.)

Stir in a little cream and/or a little butter if you'd like a richer, creamier soup. Garnish with thin slices of cooked hot dogs or with freshly made croutons.

Makes a lot. Eat as much as you can, then freeze the rest—and don't wait for Christmas Eve to make it.

Crème Crécy

Once upon a time—well, on August 26, 1346, to be exact, early in the Hundred Years' War—Edward III of England invaded Normandy and in a great battle at Crécy defeated some twenty thousand Frenchmen with his ten thousand or so English soldiers. This didn't do the English much long-term good, since their war with the French continued for generations. The most lasting thing that's supposed to have come out of the battle is the puréed carrot soup known as *crème Crécy* or *potage Crécy*. There is a legend that the soup was created more or less in the course of the battle. This conjures up visions of fighting in a carrot field and perhaps carrots being upturned as positions were dug. Maybe it became a purée because the soldiers fought too long and the carrots were overcooked. Perhaps it's all true, but there *must* have been carrot soup before 1346. Whatever the truth of all this, *crème Crécy*, even if battle-born, is a very peaceable soup.

Any carrot soup could be called a *Crécy*, but a good (and fairly French) version is:

4 medium-size carrots, scrubbed (but not peeled) and thinly sliced	4 tablespoons butter
	A good pinch of sugar
	2 cups chicken broth
1 fairly small potato, peeled and thinly sliced	Heavy cream and/or milk
	Salt and pepper
1 small onion, thinly sliced	

Stew the carrot, potato and onion slices in the butter with the pinch of sugar, covered, over a very gentle fire for 15 minutes. Stir every now and then to make sure the butter doesn't begin to brown (let alone the vegetables). Add the chicken stock and simmer until the vegetables are tender, usually 15 or 20 minutes. Purée in your usual fashion, with blender, food mill or sieve. Thin to your liking with cream and/or milk. Add salt and pepper to taste.

Serves 2 or 3.

"Thin to your liking?" What I mean is, the purée you make will be rather thick. If you thin it just a bit, it will be a hearty soup, the stick-to-your-ribs sort. If, however, you add more liquid, your *crème Crécy* will be delicate and well worthy of being a part of anyone's fancy dinner party. Either way, you can call it *crème Crécy,* since there's no one around in a position to be very authoritative about what went on at that battlefield in 1346.

Congee

Congee (also known as *jook*) is a Chinese anytime-food. We don't really have an equivalent for it: a smooth, simple gruel that can be eaten at any old time of day—for breakfast, lunch, supper or a snack—and dressed up or down according to your mood and the ingredients you have available.

Congee is hardly ever eaten plain in China, but it's good that way for moments when you can't face food—or if the people at Duke University have put you on a rice diet. (In that case, leave out the salt.) If you can stand the thought of seasoned food, add some of the things I'll tell you about after the basic recipe.

> ¼ *cup raw rice*
> *1 quart water*
> *A dash of salt*

Wash the rice thoroughly until the water that comes off it is clear. Put it into a saucepan with the water and salt. Stir so the grains will be separate. Simmer, partially covered, for 2½ to 3 hours, checking occasionally to see if you need to add more water.

At this point, you will have a rather thick gruel. If you want more of a soup effect, simply add more water. If, on the other hand, you want an even thicker finished product, cook it down quickly, uncovered.

Makes about 1 quart.

And there you are: basic *congee*. Perfect food if you feel just awful. Serve it as is or with the un-Chinese touch of a little melted butter. If you feel a little better than that, add a dash of soy sauce and/or some chopped fresh or preserved ginger, minced scallions, a drop or two of sesame oil, a little sherry or rice wine, black or white pepper, chopped fresh coriander (if you can find it), water chestnuts or other Chinese-type ingredients. (If you use any of the dried Chinese ingredients—dried scallops, shrimp, lotus seeds—add them at the beginning of the cooking.)

If you feel pretty good and up to eating more of a meal, you can add slices of raw chicken or fish for the last fifteen minutes of cooking or shreds of ham or pork for the last half hour or so.

Oyster Stew

Down on the Eastern Shore of Maryland, they make beautiful oyster stews (and they have beautiful oysters to make them with). A man down there who's famous for his regional recipes told me how to make it. His instructions involve cooking the oysters in butter until the edges curl a bit and various other such frightening directions. Since I am cowardly about these matters,

I have stuck to making oyster stew in a double boiler—with excellent results and less strain to my nervous system. Why upset yourself in the process of making something that's supposed to calm you down? The ingredients are more or less as the man told them to me, except that he sometimes adds a little minced onion. I do, too. And he may have said to add a dash of paprika. . . .

½ *pint (1 cup) oysters and their liquor*
1 cup very rich milk (or ⅔ cup milk and ⅓ cup cream)

2 tablespoons butter
Salt and pepper—and maybe paprika—to taste

Combine all the ingredients in the top of a double boiler. Heat over hot, but definitely not boiling, water. (The way to achieve this is to have the water boiling in the bottom part of the double boiler and then to turn the heat off just before you add the ingredients to the top part. At least for the purposes of this particular recipe, the water will stay hot enough to do the job.) You'll know the stew is ready when the oysters float, and by then the butter will be melted, too. There isn't quite as much rush about eating this stew as there is with the kind you make in a frying pan, but you'd better get at it within a few minutes. You'll want to, anyway.

Makes about 2 cups of stew.

And may this oyster stew stir up in you happy, soothing memories, as it does in me. Mine are of the Grand Central Oyster Bar or Susan Palmer's in New York or a little dockside place by the eastern end of the Bay Bridge in Maryland, where you can take alternate sips of martinis and oyster stew and gaze serenely at the birds around the base of the bridge.

Clam Chowder

In the clam chowder controversy, I am firmly on the side of New England. No tomatoes in my chowder, please.

This recipe came from a Boston banker who used to vacation at Cape Cod. On the first rainy day of each year's stay there, he would make this marvelous chowder, then share it with his neighbors. I was lucky enough to be on his list.

I've cut his recipe down to manageable size. The banker used to make it by the gallon and more. Just looking at that much soup, not to mention making it, might well destroy most of the calming effect of this classic chowder.

> Mince 1 small onion. Cube ¼ pound of salt pork. Cook together in a frying pan until well browned. Meanwhile, put 1 pint of shucked clams through a meat grinder—and be sure to save all the juice.
>
> Put the clams and their juice into a large pot. Add the cooked onion and salt pork. Bring to a simmer. Add 1 quart of milk. Stir while reheating, but do not allow it to boil.
>
> My banker friend didn't add potatoes, but they're quite traditional. Boil them separately first, as many as you like—I'd probably use one, or at any rate not more than two—dice them, then add to the clams with the onions and salt pork.

Even this scaled-down version makes a lot of chowder—about a quart and a half, which is much more than you could consume by yourself, I'd think. So be like that nice Bostonian and share with those who live near you. You should have a very tranquil neighborhood for a while.

Onion Soup

These are a few of the times when onion soup is the ideal food:

Breakfast
Lunch
Dinner
Midnight snacktime
When you're cold
When you've been out too late
When you've imbibed too enthusiastically

When you have the flu
When you think you might be getting the flu
When you want to pamper yourself even though you haven't been out too late, haven't been drinking at all and definitely aren't getting the flu

Some of the canned onion soups aren't bad at all, so if you wish, you can skip the preliminary section of this recipe and start at the gratinéeing part. (The homemade's better, but you don't always have time to make it at the various moments detailed above.)

1¼ cups onions, thinly sliced
2 tablespoons butter
A pinch of sugar
2 cups strong beef broth, your own or from a can
2 tablespoons white wine (optional)
Salt and pepper to taste

1 or 2 rounds of bread, preferably French, dry and well-toasted or sautéed in butter (1 piece if this soup's all for you; 2 if you're being generous with it)
Grated Swiss, Parmesan or Cheddar cheese

Cook the onions gently in the butter with the pinch of sugar until they are golden brown; stir frequently. Add the broth and the wine. (The soup's fine without the wine, but even better with it.) Cover and simmer for half an hour. Add some salt and pepper if they're needed.

Now to gratinée the soup. I'm assuming you're being greedy and having it all yourself. Pour the soup into an ovenproof bowl. Put the round of bread on the top. Sprinkle *heavily* with grated cheese—Swiss or Parmesan, preferably, but a natural Cheddar is good, too. Use so much that the bread and soup just about disappear. Brown several inches under a broiler until the cheese is melted and turning tan in spots.

Serves 1 or 2.

My idea of the perfect onion soup is what they serve at the Brasserie in New York. It's in rather large bowls, filled to the brim, and there's so much cheese that it oozes down the outside of the bowl. I don't know their recipe, but mine works out tasting a lot like theirs. I wonder if they spill as much of theirs while putting it in and taking it out of the broiler as I do. I make a terrible mess, but I've found that nestling crinkled foil around the bowl on a cookie sheet helps quite a bit.

Potato Soup

Potato soup is one of the foods to which you can develop a real devotion and even a certain dependency. It goes right straight to something elemental in you, I feel. It's foursquare and true blue and all that; something you can depend on. Practically every cookbook has a recipe for potato soup, and all the ones I've ever tried are good. This one's unusual in several ways: the potatoes are diced and never at any point mashed, there's no onion, and what in the world are bread cubes and an egg doing in a potato soup? Why, they are making the soup heartier. Also bet-

ter. This version of potato soup will warm you up and make you *stay* warm for a while, and after you eat it, you'll be far beyond soothed—you'll be absolutely sedated.

¾ cup diced, peeled potatoes	*1 egg*
1 cup boiling water	*Salt and pepper to taste*
1 cup milk	*1 tablespoon butter*
¾ cup bread cubes	

Cook the potatoes in the boiling water until tender; then add the milk (without draining off the remaining water). Heat to just below the boiling point. Add the bread cubes; then quickly stir in the egg. Cook for just a minute or two over very low heat. Add the salt, pepper and butter.

Serves 2 or 3.

If you're in more of a hurry, you can make a simpler potato soup from instant potatoes or any mashed ones you have sitting around. Cook a little minced onion in a tablespoon or two of butter until it is clear and golden. Add the instant or mashed potatoes; then stir in milk until you have the consistency you want. Heat carefully. Add salt, pepper and a dab of butter— and there you are.

Hungarian Caraway Soup

When Imre, a Hungarian friend, told me about this soup years ago, I thought he was either kidding or had been misinformed as a child about what went on in his family's kitchen. As I remember, he told me that you just take some caraway seeds and cook them with a little flour and butter and water. Just plain water. Now, how could that taste good? And yet Imre seemed to speak of this soup with yearning and nostalgia. His description stayed filed away in some dim corner of my mind, but I wasn't about to try to make the soup. In the past year or so, though, I've learned that this caraway soup *does* exist, *does* taste delicious and *does* do good things for the weary. (It must be a strictly psychological effect, because there's certainly nothing in the soup to do much for you physically. Or do you think there could be some strange property in caraway seeds that we just don't know about yet?)

I haven't seen Imre in a long time, and I don't know the exact proportions and method he had in mind, so this is my own system, evolved from several recipes I've come across. You can use beef broth instead of water if you wish, but be aware that you aren't doing the right thing; you're cheating and Americanizing.

> Start out by melting 2 tablespoons of butter until it just barely begins to brown. Add 1 tablespoon each of flour and caraway seeds and cook very slowly, stirring while the flour browns and the caraway seeds pop. And they really do! Not as spectacularly as popcorn—mostly just nice little popping noises.
>
> Then add, all at once, 1¾ cups of hot water. Stir well and simmer for 15 minutes. Add salt to taste. Imre didn't mention salt in his list of ingredients, but this soup—which is by now a lovely brew that even has some body to it—takes a good bit of it.
>
> Serves 1 or 2.

At this point, I strain out the seeds. You don't have to, but it seems to me I have enough troubles without having caraway seeds stuck in my teeth.

Bread and Herb Soup from Portugal

A wild, crazy, ridiculous soup. It doesn't even *look* like soup because it's in the Spanish-Portuguese tradition of the *sopa seca,* or dry soup—a very solid concoction. What you're really eating in this case is a bowl full of bread; but it's delicious and has come in handy for me when I'm tired but want something a little unusual.

The herbs called for are ones I happen to grow, so this has become a summertime favorite of mine. You could make it just as well with dried herbs, only in that case let them remain in the soup rather than attempting to remove them. For each sprig of fresh herb called for, substitute ¼ teaspoon of the dried and either crumble the bay leaf or leave it whole and remove it at the end.

2 cups beef stock
1 sprig fresh tarragon
1 large sprig fresh thyme
3 sprigs fresh mint
½ bay leaf
1 tablespoon butter, melted

4 slices bread, toasted and crusts
  removed, made into crumbs in
  the blender or by hand
A dash of salt
A little black pepper

Combine all the ingredients in a saucepan and bring to a boil very slowly on top of the stove. When the boiling point is reached, remove from the heat, cover and let steep for 3 minutes. Remove the herbs and pour the soup into a casserole. Bake at 350°, uncovered, for 30 minutes, or until the top is crusty and brown. Serve in a casserole to 2 or 3.

If you have a casserole that can be used on top of the stove as well as in the oven, so much the better. Use it for both parts of this operation, and if it's good-looking enough, eat your *sopa seca* right from the pot.

Chicken Soup

To begin with, you don't pronounce this chicken *soup*. The accent is on the first syllable: *chick*en soup. If you were lucky enough to have a Jewish mother, she made it every time your eyelids drooped a little—and, sure enough, it cured the droop and put sparkle back in the eye. It also tasted better, fuller, richer than any chicken soup-broth-stock in the world.

Get a nice fat stewing hen and cut it into serving pieces. If you can possibly get them, add some chicken feet—you may be able to find them at any sort of ethnic market or at a poultry farm. Put the pieces in a big pot and cover them with about 2 quarts of boiling water or, *much* better, with chicken broth.

Simmer, partly covered, for 2 hours. Then add such vegetables as a large onion, a few carrots and 2 or 3 stalks of celery. A leek or two, too, if available, and perhaps a parsnip or white turnip. Salt and pepper. Herbs and spices—anything you like. (A sprig of thyme and a bay leaf would be nice. Also, I usually stick 2 or 3 cloves into the onion. Some cooks add a dash of nutmeg.) Simmer for another hour. Strain.

This makes a lot of soup (2 quarts or so)—you won't be sorry. You can freeze what you don't need now. It also produces chicken meat—but the meat will be better if you remove it part way through the cooking, bone it and return only the bones to the pot. Later,

of course, you remove the bones and put the chicken meat back into the soup.

Don't cheat on this soup—really use the whole chicken; chicken parts won't do. Someone asked me the other day if I knew what "Depression Chicken Soup" was. I said I imagined I could guess: soup made from just the backs and maybe the wings. "No," he said glumly, "it was chicken-leg soup, and it . . ." (here he made a face) "just wasn't the same."

Chicken Corn Soup

To this day, housewives in the Pennsylvania Dutch country— even some of the chic younger ones in cities such as Lancaster— "can" prodigious quantities of Chicken Corn Soup every summer, dozens of quarts of it. I guess they just want to be sure their whole family will survive whatever traumas winter may bring.

No doubt you will want to make a smaller quantity. But I hesitate to give you a really cut-down version, because that big fat stewing chicken is the true secret of this soup. So emulate the clever Pennsylvania cooks. Take an afternoon off and make at least this much of this remarkable soup. When you're through, you'll be worn out enough to need some of it right then to revive you; then you can freeze the rest.

One 4-pound stewing chicken, cut up
3½ quarts water
Salt and pepper (perhaps a teaspoon of salt and ¼ teaspoon of pepper to start with; you can add more later)
2 stalks celery, cut up coarsely
2 carrots, cut up coarsely
1 onion, cut up coarsely
2 cups noodles
2 cups corn, cut off the cob, or frozen kernels
2 eggs, hard-boiled and chopped
2 tablespoons chopped parsley

Put the chicken, water, salt and pepper, celery, carrots and onion in a large pot. Simmer, covered, till the chicken is very tender, maybe 2 hours. Strain the broth and return it to the pot. Remove the bones and skin from the chicken, cut the meat into small pieces and put it back into the broth.

Add the noodles and corn to the broth. Boil gently until the noodles are tender. Stir in the chopped hardboiled eggs and parsley. Taste to see if more salt and pepper are needed.

Makes 5 to 6 quarts.

Some of the fancier Pennsylvania Dutch add a pinch of saffron and chill the broth, then remove the fat before adding the corn and noodles. Some of the plainer people omit the celery, carrots and onion and even the noodles. Take your pick.

Gratinée

A sound French idea for quick reviving of the weary is *gratinée*—a sort of onion soup without the onion.

For each serving, bring to a boil 1½ cups or so of good consommé or beef broth. Put into an ovenproof bowl. Top with a thickish slice of French bread, which has been lightly toasted and cut into 4 pieces. Top that with a hefty sprinkling of grated Gruyère cheese. Bake at 425° until the cheese is melted and browning and bubbling. Remove from the oven and let cool for 3 or 4 minutes while you beat 1 egg with 2 or 3 tablespoons of port or perhaps sherry. Push the bread cubes aside a bit with a spoon, using your left hand. (If you're left-handed, you'll know to switch these instructions.) With your right hand, spoon out some of the broth and beat it into the egg-sherry combination. Then stir this mixture into the soup through the hole the spoon in your left hand is maintaining. Stir slowly; otherwise you will capsize the bread. This is just a little tricky, but it's fun and not really hard.

Read on for two other versions of this way to accomplish with ease a quick restoration of strength and good humor.

Zuppa Pavese

In Italy, the *gratinée* of the previous recipe becomes *zuppa pavese,* and the egg is poached, not beaten, while the bread becomes crisp through being fried instead of toasted. Also, the Italians don't seem to feel the need for wine in their version.

Heat about 1½ cups of good beef broth in a rather wide saucepan or a frying pan. Break an egg gently into the simmering broth and poach until the white is set. Lift the egg out carefully with a slotted spoon and put it into a soup plate or bowl. Add the broth, then a large slice of Italian bread that you've cut in half and fried in butter until crisp. Top with grated Parmesan or Romano cheese.

A delightful lunch—and a strength-giver that really works.

Mrs. Rittenour's Reviver

Elizabeth ("Diddy") Rittenour, my mother's cousin (my cousin, too), has a more direct and simpler approach to the *gratinée-zuppa pavese* sort of thing. She just heats up a can of consommé and combines it with a beaten egg and a teaspoon or two of sherry. She tells me that it kept her going during the aftermath of a bad car accident. It's kept me going in some tough times, too.

Cheddar Cheese Soup

This soup started out to be an attempt to copy the cheese soup at Emily Shaw's Restaurant in Pound Ridge, New York. By now, it's been so long since I've been there that I can't quite remember what theirs is like. All I know is that while it may not be quite the same as this one, it couldn't possibly be any better or any more perfect for a cold day. (It's not so bad on a warm day, either.)

1 small onion or 3 fat scallions, chopped
1½ tablespoons butter
1 tablespoon flour
1 cup milk
1 cup chicken broth, homemade or a good canned brand such as College Inn

½ cup or more Cheddar cheese, grated or shredded
½ cup white wine (optional)
2 tablespoons heavy cream
A few grains of nutmeg
Salt and freshly ground black pepper to taste

Cook the onion or scallions in the butter until soft. Add the flour, then the milk and chicken broth. Simmer for 20 minutes. At this point, you can put the soup

through a sieve or run it in the blender if you want to get rid of visible evidence of the onion or scallion. But you certainly don't have to.

Now add the cheese and, if you want, the wine. (The wine adds a sophistication that you may not feel like having at the moment.) Cook and stir a few minutes more, until the cheese is melted. Taste to see if the soup could use more cheese. Stir in the heavy cream and season with nutmeg and salt and pepper (freshly ground black pepper makes quite a difference here).

Serves 1 to 3.

This cheese soup is not as aggressively "hearty" as some others you may have tried. It's fairly light and delicate, especially if you add the wine. If you want it heavier, use 2 tablespoons of flour and more cheese.

Canned cheese soup isn't very much like this. It can be helped along by adding butter, wine, milk, cream, a chicken bouillon cube and some nutmeg. But if you're going to go to all that trouble, you might as well make your own soup from the beginning.

Hot Borscht

Here's one of the best warmers for a freezing day, and one of the most comforting foods for any occasion.

This tastes like what the Russian Tea Room in New York, a favorite spot of mine since I was a teenager, calls Hot Borscht. Actually, though, it's closer to the Russian soup called *s'chee*, since it contains no beets. This is basically Marian Tracy's recipe, as given in *The Peasant Cookbook* (Hanover House, 1955), a marvelous book I wish I could get a copy of again (mine burned up in a fire). Mrs. Tracy calls it *s'chee*. I'm giving you the full amounts for enough soup to serve six to eight, since it's so good and since you could freeze part of it. If you want to make less, you can divide the ingredients by two or four.

1 head cabbage, slivered (don't use the stalk)
2 carrots, scraped and sliced
2 stalks celery, sliced
1 whole turnip, peeled and cubed
6 cups beef bouillon
1 can Italian tomato paste
Salt and pepper
2 onions, peeled and sliced
1 clove garlic, pressed or minced
3 tablespoons bacon fat
3 medium-sized potatoes, peeled and cubed
Sour cream
Chopped fresh dill or dried dill weed
Chopped fresh parsley

Simmer the cabbage, carrots, celery and turnip in the bouillon for a few minutes. Add the tomato paste and a little salt and pepper. Simmer for 2 or 3 hours. Sauté the onions and garlic briefly in the bacon fat and add to the soup along with the potatoes. Cook for about a half hour longer.

To warm 6 to 8 freezing people, serve in a large tureen with a bowl of sour cream on the side and with the dill and parsley mixed in a little bowl, ready to sprinkle on top. Each soup-eater puts a large spoonful of sour cream on top of the serving of soup, then sprinkles on the herbs.

When I was a teenager and ate more—and restaurant food cost less—I usually had this as the second course of a feast of a lunch at the Russian Tea Room. Today, the feast for me consists of *borscht* with *piroschki* (crisp, meat-filled puff-paste turnovers) and a special rum-chocolate-macaroon pastry.

Cottage Cheese Soup

Once upon a time, my milkman talked me into signing up for a big special: large aluminum tumblers at a very low price. I thought they'd be good to have for bathroom glasses, etc., and indeed they were. But there was a catch. Each tumbler arrived filled with cottage cheese, and a new one was delivered every other day. We were inundated with cottage cheese. About the only benefit of all this, aside from acquiring more tumblers than we could use, was that in the course of desperate searching for new ways to use cottage cheese, I found a wonderful soup. I've always served it hot, but it should be just as good (and even more refreshing) cold.

2 tablespoons butter	½ teaspoon celery seed or celery salt
2 tablespoons minced onion	
1 tablespoon flour	Salt and pepper
2 cups milk	1 tablespoon minced pimiento or blanched green pepper
1 cup cottage cheese	

Melt the butter and sauté the onion in it until soft but not brown. Blend in the flour and slowly add the milk. Now add a half-cup or so of this mixture, which is just a very thin white sauce, to the cottage cheese and zip them together in a blender until smooth. Stir this back into the rest of the soup, add the seasonings and stir until the mixture is hot but not boiling. Stir in the pimiento or green pepper just before serving.

Serves 2 or 3.

The tumblers have long since disappeared, as things seem to in my house, but the cottage cheese soup has become a fixture.

Mixed Fruit Soup

It takes moral courage to taste, let alone cook, fruit soup for the first time. Be brave—you'll probably like it. The French, the Scandinavians, the Hungarians, the Germans, the English (to some extent) and many other groups have been enjoying fruit soups for centuries. The average American is lagging behind. Come on in; the fruit soup's fine.

Some fruit soups play it straight. Apples, say, are cooked with chicken broth and, perhaps, onion, then puréed just as though they were potatoes or some other more usual soup ingredient. Others feature wine and/or spices and taste unlike anything you've ever tried. And still others are so heavily sweetened that they taste like dessert. Most fruit soups are served cold, and they can be tremendously cooling and cheering on a hot day. Some are better hot, and they're warming when the occasion demands.

This hot (or cold), winy, spicy version might be a good place to start an exploration of the fruit soups. It's rather a gorgeous thing. My mother used to serve it occasionally as a first course at dinner parties—to great critical acclaim.

1 package (11 ounces or so) of
   mixed dried fruit
3 cups water
¼ cup red wine
¼ cup sugar

½ cinnamon stick
½ teaspoon dried orange peel or
   1 teaspoon finely grated fresh
Whipped cream or sour cream for
   garnish

Packages of dried fruit vary. If yours doesn't include peaches, you might want to add 1 or 2 fresh ones, peeled and sliced. Cut up the dried fruit coarsely. Follow the directions on the package for any soaking and cooking, but use 3 cups of water and the wine and add the sugar, cinnamon stick and orange peel. Cook until very tender.

Remove the cinnamon stick and any prune pits there might be. Then if you like, you can purée the soup, but I don't like to. The soup has much more character if you don't.

Reheat and serve topped with a spoonful of whipped cream or sour cream.

This utterly delicious soup will serve 3 or 4 as a first course. For you alone, it can provide dinner—with a bonus left over for breakfast.

P.S. It's wonderful cold, too.

Avgolemono

Avgolemono is the Greek version of the broth-and-egg soups that turn up in place after place around the world, from the egg drop soup of China to the *gratinée* of France (page 20). Like all these soups, *avgolemono* is soothing, but it has something else going for it: the wonderful combination of egg and lemon that is what makes hollandaise and *béarnaise* and even mayonnaise taste so marvelous.

Most *avgolemono*-makers have rice in their soup, and I'll tell you how to do it that way, too. But I prefer a riceless soup in this case: it's quicker, less fattening and, I think, just as good. It chills well, too, and it's hard to imagine the rice version served cold.

3 cups very rich, strong chicken broth

2 eggs

Juice of 1 lemon

Parsley, minced, for garnish (optional but nice)

Salt and pepper

Bring the chicken broth to a boil. Beat the eggs and lemon juice thoroughly in a blender or with a beater and bowl. While still blending or beating, add a couple of ladlefuls of hot broth; then remove the pan of broth from the fire and stir in the egg-lemon mixture. Pour with your left hand and stir constantly with your right (if you're right handed). I usually find the soup just to my liking at this stage, but if you want it thicker, cook and stir over a very low fire for a minute or two more —just be sure not to let it boil or it will curdle, and then you might as well throw it away. Don't even let it get near a simmer. Add salt and pepper to taste. Sprinkle with parsley.

Serves 2 to 4.

To make the classic *avgolemono* with rice, use ¼ cup of rice and 4 cups of broth instead of 3. Cook for 20 minutes (until the rice is done), then continue as directed.

Other kinds of broth can be used, also. Beef broth's good, and lamb broth's fabulous in this recipe, in case you have thought to make some with those old lamb bones you have lying around in your freezer.

When the soup is served chilled, minced fresh mint is a refreshing substitute for the parsley.

Pumpkin and Apple Soup

Since this soup is made of such down-to-earth, harvest-home things, you might expect it to taste elemental and hearty. Not at all. It's light and subtle and a charmer all the way.

1 cup pumpkin, peeled and diced A pinch of marjoram
1 apple, peeled and diced Salt and pepper
1 small onion, peeled and diced Heavy cream
2 cups chicken broth

Simmer the pumpkin, apple and onion in the chicken broth along with the marjoram and some salt and pepper until everything is soft. This takes quite a while, perhaps 45 minutes for pumpkin in fairly small dice. Run through a blender, food mill or sieve. Thin the soup down with heavy cream until it's a consistency you like. Correct the seasoning. Reheat gently without bringing to the boil.

Even better, chill the soup thoroughly after turning it into a purée. Thin it down with cream or even milk for one of the best cold soups possible. Make it a little thinner than normal, since it will thicken slightly as it chills.

Serves 1 to 3.

This is such a small amount of pumpkin that you can probably sneak it out of the inside of your jack-o'-lantern (before it's lit, of course). Or if it's not Halloween or you can't find a tiny pumpkin, use any winter squash.

Madzoon Soup

One of my closest friends still mumbles occasionally—and in quite an irascible way—about the *madzoon* soup I talked her into trying years ago at the Golden Horn, a marvelous middle-Eastern (mostly Armenian) restaurant that unfortunately no longer exists in New York. I loved this yogurt-barley-mint soup, and still do; she *hated* it. To me it's soothing; to her it was down-right irritating. So just be aware that this (by my way of thinking) magnificent creation won't be everyone's cup of soup.

This recipe has evolved from several versions I've seen in print, and seems to me to be just like the one I remember at the Golden Horn. (I really miss that restaurant. The last time I arranged to meet someone there for lunch, there was no restaurant at all—no building, in fact; just, in typical New York fashion, a large hole in the ground.)

3 tablespoons barley (the real thing, not egg barley, which is a noodle)

5 cups water—or make 1 cup of this be chicken broth

1 small onion, minced

2 tablespoons butter

1 teaspoon dried mint or 1 table-spoon fresh mint

1 cup plain yogurt (madzoon)

Salt and pepper

Wash the barley, then cook it gently in the water for 1½ hours, or until it's tender. Meanwhile, cook the onion in the butter until it's transparent and add to the barley mixture. Crumble or chop the mint, removing any stems, and add it, too.

Let the soup cool to lukewarm, then stir in the yogurt. Add salt and pepper to taste.

Either reheat to just below the boiling point or chill and serve cold to 4 or 5. Both ways are good, but cold's best, I think.

If you're like me and take a liking to this soup, you'll probably find yourself making it frequently and keeping it chilled, ready to give you a quick, refreshing pickup whenever you need it. You'll probably end up making a double recipe of it, in fact.

Vichyssoise

Good vichyssoise is such a treat. Bad vichyssoise . . . awful.
I ordered vichyssoise in a dubious restaurant once. The waitress
raised an eyebrow and said, "You know it's just cold potato soup,
don't you?" She was right. I think what they served as vichyssoise
was last night's mashed potatoes, thinned down—and they hadn't
even gotten all the lumps out. As for canned vichyssoise—even
if it doesn't give you botulism, it certainly won't give you much
of an idea of what the real thing is like.

I've tried dozens of vichyssoise recipes, including the ones that
have you using two or three kinds of cream (which seems pretty
silly), trying to find the "perfect" vichyssoise. To me this means
one that tastes right, has the right consistency, isn't too hard to
make and can be made with scallions when leeks are too expensive to even think about. Here it is.

*1 bunch scallions or 2 large
leeks, the white part only in
either case, minced*
¾ cup onions, thinly sliced
3 tablespoons butter
*2 medium-size potatoes, peeled
and thinly sliced*

2 cups strong chicken broth
½ cup heavy cream
½ cup milk
Salt and white pepper
A few grains of nutmeg (optional)
Minced chives, for garnish

Cook the scallions or leeks and onions very gently in
the butter for 5 minutes or more, until they are the
usual "soft but not browned." Add the potatoes and stir
around until they're coated with butter. Add the
chicken broth. Simmer, covered, until the potatoes are
soft—20 minutes should suffice. Cool slightly. Purée in
the blender or put through a food mill or sieve. Add

the cream and milk. (It seems to me you should be able to use light cream instead of this combination, but the soup is so good as is that I haven't yet tried this substitution.) Season with salt, pepper and nutmeg. Use a little more salt than you think you'd need, just a little white pepper and a small speck of nutmeg. Chill very thoroughly, till the soup is downright icy. Serve with minced chives sprinkled on top. (Sometimes I mix them in the soup before chilling, to give a flavor of chive throughout the soup.)

This will give you about one quart of vichyssoise, which should admirably soothe one person over a period of several hours.

Quick Vichyssoise Base

This is a good trick to know about. It's practically effortless, inexpensive and makes a vichyssoise almost as good as the kind you make from scratch.

Buy a box of Knorr Swiss Leek Soupmix. Follow the directions they give you for vichyssoise. When you're through, you'll have a thick base. Strain it if you want to remove the visible pieces of green leek. Chill well. Then, when you want some vichyssoise, all you have to do is to put some of this base into a bowl, thin it down with cold milk and sprinkle with chives.

In case the Knorr people stop giving the instructions for vichyssoise, I'd better tell you what to do. This is my version of what's on the box currently. Pour the contents of the box into a saucepan. Add 2½ cups of water. Stir constantly while bringing to a boil; then turn the heat down, cover partially and simmer for 10 minutes. Now add 2 cups of milk and rapidly bring to the boil again. Allow to cool at room temperature, stirring from time to time, then continue as above—in other words, use this thick mixture as a vichyssoise base, straining it, chilling it, adding milk when serving.

Gazpacho

Gazpacho is one of the few soothing cold soups that can be made on the spur of the moment and consumed right away. Vichyssoise and so many others have to be made ahead of time and then chilled. For *gazpacho,* all you need is to have cold tomato juice and certain vegetables on hand; then you serve it with an ice cube or two floating in it, which is quite *de rigueur* in *gazpacho* circles, even in Spain. You might give it a few minutes in the freezer to help the chilling along.

For this recipe, I am simply going to have to borrow from my earlier book *Impromptu Cooking* (Atheneum, 1973), since the *gazpacho* given there is, to me, the best possible one. It was one of the few places in that book where I was fairly explicit—though I did attach a list of other items that could be added. We'll leave those out this time.

1 large cucumber, peeled	*½ cup olive oil*
4 large tomatoes (or even canned tomatoes)	*2 tablespoons wine vinegar*
	A dash of Tabasco sauce
1 green pepper	*Salt and pepper to taste*
1 medium onion	*Croutons for garnish*
3 to 4 cups tomato juice	

Chop the cucumber, tomatoes, green pepper and onion into good-sized hunks. Reserve a small amount of each to mince finely for garnish. Blend the rest, adding tomato juice as needed. Run through the blender in several batches and turn the blender on for just a moment or two each time.

Pour each batch into a big bowl. Add the olive oil, vinegar, Tabasco, salt and pepper. Then, while stirring, add more tomato juice until you get the consistency you want—fairly solid, but still definitely a soup. Chill . . . serve with the reserved minced vegetables and croutons and add as desired.

Serves 5 or 6.

It's hard to figure out why *gazpacho* is so incredibly refreshing. It isn't just its coldness. Do you think it could have something to do with all the ingredients being so good for you?

Cold Cream of Nothing Soup

This soup is named in honor of one of the specialties of the cook at a boarding school I attended—Creamed Nothing. At least, that was the name the students gave (as a matter of fact, I think I may have been the one who thought of this name) to a remarkable main dish that seemed to consist of nothing but white sauce on toast. It often appeared as part of the cook's famous all-white dinner: mushroom soup, Creamed Nothing, cauliflower, boiled and peeled potatoes and for dessert, vanilla ice cream. A more horrid meal you have never encountered. But Cream of Nothing Soup is different. It's good.

2 cups well-flavored chicken broth

2 eggs

1 tablespoon sherry

1 teaspoon lemon juice

¼ cup heavy cream

Salt and pepper to taste

Bring the chicken broth just to a boil. Beat the egg, sherry and lemon juice (in a blender, preferably) and while still beating, add to them a ladleful of broth. Now quickly stir the egg mixture back into the rest of the broth. Remove from the heat. Let cool slightly. Add the heavy cream. Add salt and pepper, if needed. (White pepper, perhaps, to continue the no-color theme.) Chill very thoroughly.

If there's some special seasoning you feel a yen for—curry, cinnamon or anything at all—add it to the eggs.

Serves 1 or 2.

This is a little like a cold *Avgolemono* but different enough, and fine enough, to stand on its own. Cold Cream of Nothing is superb, and I feel a little guilty about giving it the same name as that schoolgirls' nightmare.

Cold Cucumber Soup

"Cool as a cucumber," they say. "Cooling as cold cucumber soup," they might as well also say, though perhaps this projected cliché doesn't have quite enough zing to it. The soup does, though; it's zingy as all get-out, but with pure cucumber taste, not a lot of extraneous flavors.

1 cucumber, peeled and thinly sliced (save a slice or two for garnish)
⅓ cup minced onion

1 tablespoon butter
1½ cups chicken broth
¼ to ½ cup heavy cream
Salt and white pepper to taste

Cook the cucumber and onion gently in the butter for 5 or 10 minutes, or until they are fairly soft but not at all browned. Add the chicken broth. (If you're making it from chicken bouillon cubes, use 2 of them to 1½ cups of water.) Purée in the blender until the cucumber seeds disappear. Return to the pot and simmer for a few minutes; cool. Add the cream—enough to make the soup the consistency you want. (The amount varies with the size cucumber you use.) Season with salt and white pepper. Chill thoroughly.

    Serves 1 or 2.

If you happen to be on a low-carbohydrate diet, take a look at the ingredients of this soup—it will do more for you than vichyssoise for the duration.

Senegalese Soup

Senegalese Soup is also known as *crème Singhalese*. It's also known as cold cream of curry soup or cold chicken and curry soup, so you get the idea of what it's like. To look at it, you might think it a very slightly tan, chiveless vichyssoise, but when you taste it you'll learn better. Both are cold and light and good, but they're continents apart in flavor.

Recipes for this bliss-giving soup vary widely. There are some with carrots, leeks, celery and all sorts of things like that and even one with puréed peas. I like a simpler way. If you use good chicken broth as a base, you don't need the carrots and so forth. As for the pea purée, I've tried adding it and it's nice but, to me, totally unnecessary. I do use sautéed onion, though, since it gives a different flavor from the broth, and a good one. The apple is important, but you can have a good Senegalese without it, too.

1 *small onion, chopped*
1 *small apple, peeled and sliced*
2 *tablespoons butter*
1½ *teaspoons or less curry powder (Madras, if possible)*
2 *cups chicken broth*
1 *teaspoon arrowroot or cornstarch*
*Cooked chicken, diced or sliv-
  ered, a little (maybe ¼ cup)*
1 *cup heavy cream*
Salt and white pepper

Cook the onion and apple in the butter very slowly
until they are soft, but don't let them brown at all. Stir
in the curry powder and cook and stir for 2 or 3 minutes. Mix a little of the chicken broth with the arrowroot. Add this and the rest of the broth to the onion-
apple mixture. Simmer for a few minutes until the soup
thickens a bit. Add the cooked chicken now or save it,
well-slivered, for garnish later. Purée the soup in a
blender or through a food mill or sieve. Add the cream,
salt and white pepper. Chill thoroughly.
   Serves 2 or 3.

Today I learned that a Senegalese Soup doesn't really require
chicken. I was giving this recipe a final testing and was well
into it when I discovered that someone had evidently eaten the
little bit of cooked chicken I had set aside especially for this
soup. (Wait till I catch whoever it was!) The Senegalese I made
tasted about the same.
   When my parents and I had a Jersey cow, one of the ways we
used up the milk was in a pseudo-Senegalese. It involved Lip-
ton's chicken noodle soup, a gallon of milk, curry powder and
chives, a brief boiling and the use of a blender. I can't remember
the exact details, and I don't happen to have a spare gallon of
milk to play around with, but I'm sure you can figure it out if
you have a similar problem. It certainly does use up milk, and
on hot days it's nice to have it there, chilled and waiting, when
you come in from taking care of that cow.

MEAT, CHICKEN AND FISH

WHY WOULD YOU ever want meat, chicken or fish when you're beset by moods?

Well, first of all, perhaps a craving for protein might be the physical cause of your moodiness. (If so, don't forget eggs and cheese, too.)

But from there, we have to go to all the vague psychic and psychological reasons for a craving for meat, poultry or fish. Some of these dishes are nostalgic—for those who want a quick (if, happily, temporary) return to the womb. Some are elegant— for moments when you're feeling down at the heels. Some (steak, as an example) are such a straight shot of protein that they're mainly for strength and courage.

In other words, meat, poultry and fish can fulfill a lot of needs —these and others. Most of them are mentioned along with the recipes, but for quick finding of the very thing for the immediate moment, consult the special Mood Index on page 241.

Lobscouse

An easy way for me to get sighs of delight from everyone in my house is to serve them Lobscouse. This is an old-time sailor's stew. Supposedly it could be thrown together when the provisions got low toward the end of a voyage, just about the time scurvy was setting in. Versions of Lobscouse turn up all over the world. (Those ships did get around.) Mine has only salt pork, beef, potatoes and onions, and would probably be good (at the very end of the voyage) without the beef. Others, presumably to be made when not long out of port, include cabbage and green beans and such; you might as well just call these beef stews. The *real* Lobscouse:

1 pound stewing beef, cubed
¼ pound salt pork, cubed
Water to cover
2 potatoes, peeled and cut in
  chunks

1 onion, peeled and coarsely cut
Salt and pepper

Cover the beef and salt pork with water. Simmer until the beef is almost tender. If the cubes of meat are large, this can take 2 hours; smaller pieces cook in a much shorter time. Add the potatoes and onions and the salt and pepper. (Go easy on the salt: the salt pork may have provided enough.) Cook 20 minutes or so more, until the potatoes are tender.

Now the Lobscouse is ready to serve, but you have to decide (in fact, it would help if you had decided a while ago) whether you want it to be liquid enough to serve in soup bowls or as thick as a regular stew. For a soup effect, simply use more water—add some now, if it's needed. (No beef broth, please, just water.)

However, if you want to make the Lobscouse thicker, just boil it down quickly; some of the water will evaporate, and the potatoes will disintegrate somewhat and help the thickening process.

Serves 3 or 4.

It may help you to understand how I feel about Lobscouse if I tell you this. A year or two ago, I tore around all day getting things ready for some people who were coming for dinner. I had an elaborate meal, featuring an especially sumptuous sort of beef stroganoff, planned. Late in the afternoon, I learned that our prospective guests were sick and couldn't come. At that point, I was exhausted, disgusted and generally disgruntled. "To hell with it," I said, and threw the steak cubes that had been going to be stroganoff into a pot and made Lobscouse out of them. Just smelling the pot while the Lobscouse was cooking made me feel better, and we ended up having a happy family dinner, with even the cook—me—smiling again.

Creamed Chipped Beef on Toast

My father thinks creamed chipped beef is, next to milk and crackers, the most soothing food there could possibly be. I was visiting him this past year when he discovered you could buy chipped beef, all creamed and ready to go, in little frozen pouches. From that moment on, we stopped going out to restaurants for dinner, a practice I had been thoroughly enjoying. After that, it was creamed chipped beef on toast at home every night for him—and for me, something else from the frozen food counter.

My own feelings about chipped beef? I can't stand the stuff. Some of my less happy childhood memories involve being left behind at the lunch table, all by myself, with orders to stay there until I ate it all up. Misery. Fortunately, though, we had a dog, a wonderful English setter named Chester, who liked chipped beef almost as much as my father. Eventually, I'd get good old Chester into the dining room and sneak my plate down onto the floor, and in half a minute my troubles would be over.

Here, so I am told, is how to make creamed chipped beef, for you or your dog.

First, make a cream sauce by melting 1½ tablespoons of butter, adding 1½ tablespoons of flour, then 1 cup of milk. Stir and simmer until the sauce thickens, then add about ¼ cup of chipped beef. Season with salt and pepper—but taste carefully first, as chipped beef is very salty. Serve on buttered toast.

That's the classic creamed chipped beef, and the way most people like it best. You can, however, add ½ cup of room temperature sour cream to the finished sauce or you can sauté 1 or 2 tablespoons of minced onion in the butter when you begin to make the sauce. Either of these should help. A dash of nutmeg, too.

Serves 1 or 2.

I wonder why I didn't like creamed chipped beef as a child and won't even try it now? I should have realized that it was practically the same as something I thought sounded very romantic and exciting: the *pemmican* of the Indians. I think the trouble probably was that there was sherry in the sauce, and I just wasn't up to sherry in my food yet. I had the same problem with mushroom-and-sherry sauce in those days.

Steak

There are times when absolutely nothing but a steak will do. True, you have to exert yourself to eat it, but when a craving for solid meat takes over, it's worth the effort. Steak is especially profitable for moments of mental tiredness or when you have an ordeal of some sort coming up and very little strength with which to face it. That, I suppose, is what you might call "mood-prevention."

For a steak that will truly sustain you, buy the best individual piece of meat you can find: go to a butcher shop that specializes in prime meats if you can and tell them you want a really beautiful steak to serve one person. (If you live near Upper Montclair, New Jersey, Mac's Laurel Market is the place.) You'll probably be given a strip steak or whatever they call it in your locality . . . perhaps a "New York steak," if you live somewhere other than New York. To make the eating easier, have the bone removed.

A steak to serve one will undoubtedly be too thin to broil in the kitchen; it can successfully be grilled over a very hot charcoal fire. What you have to do is to pan-broil or sauté the steak if, that is, you want it to be rarish on the inside, but with a brown crust. Don't be alarmed at the thought of frying a steak; most of those lovely "broiled" steaks you get in fine restaurants have actually been cooked on top of the stove in a pan.

The system I give you is my own. Most steak cooks would tell you either to have the pan very hot and use no shortening or to cook the steak slowly and gently in a little fat. My way smokes up the kitchen, if not the whole house, but it turns out a superb steak.

First, if you have a kitchen fan, turn it on full blast. Or open some doors and windows. Then heat a frying pan

—preferably an iron skillet—till it is very, very hot. Throw in about ½ tablespoon of butter, then add your steak. Cook until the meat is beautifully brown on the bottom, which will be in roughly 1 minute. Turn the meat over and repeat. (For more well-done meat, turn the heat down and cook for 1 or 2 more minutes on each side.)

Take the pan off the stove immediately to stop the production of smoke. Put the steak on a hot plate, add a dab of butter and grope your way out of the kitchen.

Middle-American Pot Dinner

The very thing for when you want something easy to make but warming, filling and essentially down-home. This is one of the many marvelous dishes that have come out of the European hodgepodge of peoples who settled the American Middle West. Actually, probably not just one but many of the good pioneer cooks out there thought it up independently of each other. It's a very sensible dish.

4 or 5 slices of bacon　　*1 or 2 potatoes, thinly sliced*
½ pound beef round or chuck,　*Salt and pepper*
*　cut into thin strips*　　*Water*
1 or 2 onions, thinly sliced

Use a heavy pot for this—a small Dutch oven would be perfect. Line the pot with the slices of bacon, cut in half or in thirds if you want. Now come the strips of beef. Top these with the onions, then the potatoes. Sprinkle with a little salt and pepper. Cook over brisk heat for two or three minutes, then gently add water just up to the level of the onions. Cover and cook over low heat or in a 325° oven for 45 minutes, or until the meat is tender. (Stick a fork down through the potatoes and onions into the meat to find out.)

There should be no discernible water left in the pot. If there is, boil it off. In fact, this pot dinner is especially delicious if the bacon lining the bottom is almost burned—but do note that word *almost.*

Serves 1 or 2.

Corned Beef Hash

There was a boy I used to see a good bit of when I was in my late teens. The romance fizzled out, but when I later saw him now and then, he would say, "You know, I've never forgotten that wonderful corned beef hash you made." Maybe he'd never forgotten it, but I had! I finally figured out that what he meant was Broadcast corned beef hash, straight from the can. I had put it in a pan, made four indentations in it, slipped a raw egg in each and baked it until the eggs were set. I can do better than that these days, and I really do feel that the corned beef hash I make now might be *worth* remembering.

Sometimes it's still the canned variety, in which case I fry some minced onions and green peppers in butter; then combine them with the hash and maybe a teaspoon of prepared mustard and cook the mixture on top of the stove till the bottom's well browned and crusty. But at other times I start from scratch:

1 small onion, minced
1 tablespoon minced green pepper (optional)
3 tablespoons butter
1 cup chopped corned beef (more
 or less)—leftover or from a can

1 cup boiled, pared and chopped
 potatoes
2 tablespoons beef stock or heavy
 cream
Salt and pepper
½ teaspoon prepared mustard

Cook the onions (and the green pepper if you're using it) in 1 tablespoon of the butter until they are soft but not brown. Combine in a bowl with the corned beef, potatoes, stock or cream, salt, pepper and mustard. Chill until it firms up. Melt the remaining 2 tablespoons of the butter in a frying pan. Add the hash mixture. Cook over low heat until the bottom is brown and a crust has formed.

This should serve two, but it can be stretched to serve more by using more potatoes.

When I say that at times I "start from scratch," I'm including the times I even corn my own beef. But that's a major production and not soothing in the least.

Red Flannel Hash

Anyone who likes corned beef hash at all should try red flannel hash. It's prettier, tastier and more calming. The "red" of the title comes from the color added by beets, the "flannel" from the smoothness the beets impart. This is very much a New England specialty—they know how to live up there.

For the simplest red flannel hash, just add 1 cup of cooked, chopped beets (canned, if you want to make things easy) to either a can of corned beef hash or to the hash mixture in the previous recipe. Continue as you would for the regular hash.

But even better is a red flannel hash that includes salt pork, ¼ pound of it, diced, cooked by itself until brown, then added to the hash mixture before it goes into the frying pan. Use some of the fat from the salt pork to cook the hash, if you like. I like.

Veal Isis

Isis was an Egyptian goddess. She was also a regally beautiful, quite mystic black cat who lived with my friends Hope and Alan Peek. Here, in Hope's words, is Veal Isis.

"Veal scallops (3 per person)   *Butter*
Fresh basil, chopped   *1 cup water*
Grated lemon rind   *1 bouillon cube*
Salt and pepper   *Lemon juice*

"Cut and flatten veal so that each piece is very thin and approximately 2½ by 5 inches. Sprinkle with chopped basil, grated lemon rind, salt and pepper. Roll up the long way and tie.

"Brown veal in butter. Add water and a bouillon cube (not too strong or it will be salty when reduced) so that it comes half way over veal. Squeeze on lemon juice. Cover and simmer 1 hour.

"Put veal on platter. Remove string. Reduce sauce in pan to approximately 1 tablespoon per veal roll. Spoon sauce over veal. Allow to cool or put in refrigerator.

"Serve only on full-moon nights of summer, accompanied by any good California Pinot Chardonnay, Bibb lettuce salad, freshly baked bread, fresh peaches, however you will, and love."

Veal Isis is pretty to look at, refreshing to the palate and the soul and altogether the loveliest summer dish I know of—full-moon nights or no.

Broiled Lamb Chops

After an exhausting day at Montreal's Expo, my husband and I returned to our hotel. I was not only bone-tired, but also coming down with a bad cold, and I guess I was being rather difficult. I had in mind certain food I wanted and I wouldn't settle for anything else. Also, I wouldn't stir any farther than the hotel dining room, which claimed to be a French restaurant.

The things I was craving were simple: a martini, some vichyssoise and one lamb chop. But my ordering these things devastated this so-called "home of superb French cuisine," and the things they served me devastated me. I wanted the martini to be dry and to have a twist of lemon. I got a light brown, over-vermouthed martini with not only an olive, but some of the juice in which it had been packed. The vichyssoise was tasteless, lumpy and lukewarm. The lamb chop was the saddest thing of all. The waiter, captain and maître d' had gone into horrified consultation at the thought of someone wanting one unadorned lamb chop. It took a good bit of somewhat irascible persuasion to convince these haughty personages that since they had lamb chops on the menu they could manage to serve me just one, all by itself, without the embellishments (*duchesse* potatoes, and so on) they considered necessary. I didn't even want to look at extraneous food.

When I saw and tasted the lamb chop I wished they had stuck to their ridiculous refusal to serve it. It was about three-eighths of an inch thick, the meat of it was as big around as a silver dollar and it was fried crisp, utterly overdone and dry.

I almost cried. What I had in mind was more like the luscious lamb chops Dione Lucas used to serve when she had a restaurant in New York. Or the ones I cook myself when I'm feeling wildly extravagant:

> Start with a big, thick loin chop that you've obtained from a reputable butcher. (If you're going to spend the amount of money involved in lamb chops, spend a little more and get really good ones.)
>
> Rub a little olive oil into both sides of the chop. If it's a 1½-inch-thick chop, broil on a rack for 4 minutes on one side, then 4 minutes on the other. Cook a thicker chop a little longer. If the chop isn't brown enough to suit you toward the end of the cooking time, move it closer to the fire. (You only need to make one side an appetizing brown; the other will be hidden on the plate and will taste just as good.)
>
> Serve with a little of the cooked-off fat from the broiler or a slice of butter. Or, best of all, with chive butter which you've made at least an hour or two ahead: Soften 2 tablespoons of butter. Add 1 teaspoon of chopped chives, a few drops of lemon juice, salt and pepper to taste; chill well.

A thinner chop should be pan-cooked, not hard-fried as at that awful Montreal restaurant. Just gently cooked in a small amount of butter.

I must try Montreal food again sometime. My friends have epicurean feasts there. I've only had experiences such as this one in pretentious, so-called French restaurants that served food no self-respecting hash-house would dare turn out. No, in all fairness, I must say that I did have one magnificent meal in Montreal—a Chinese one at Ruby Foo's.

Absolutely Plain Baked Breast of Lamb

Absolutely plain, that is, if you don't count salt and pepper. There come times in most lives when what's wanted is something crisp and very plain, when there isn't sufficient energy available to do any deep-frying or other messing-about in the kitchen. All you need for plain, crisp, baked lamb is time. (Though you do have to summon up the strength to turn the lamb every now and then.) The taste is pure lamb. (Have you ever tasted lamb that has no other flavor—except salt and pepper—added to it? You should!)

> If you want *very* crisp lamb, cut the breasts into separate ribs. Otherwise, leave in larger pieces. Put in a large pan, sprinkle lightly with salt and pepper. Bake at 350° for about 1½ to 2 hours, turning roughly every half hour. (Smaller rib pieces—shorter cooking time.)

You may find these called lamb ribs or lamb riblets instead of breast of lamb, but these names all mean the same thing. Sometimes a portion of the meat will be boneless. Pay no attention—just cook in the same way. This cut of lamb is usually very fatty, but don't worry, most of the grease melts, and you just leave it behind in the pan.

Someday the world will catch on to breast of lamb, and it will be as expensive as pork spareribs. In the meantime, eat it often.

Absolutely Plain Spareribs

These are exactly the same as the Absolutely Plain Baked Breast of Lamb in the preceding recipe, with the obvious exception that you use pork spareribs instead of breast of lamb. Fond as I am of spareribs cooked in a Southern-type barbecue sauce or in a Polynesian marinade, I think these ribs are really better. Follow the instructions for the lamb, but use a lower oven temperature, 300° or 325°. If you're so accustomed to sauced spareribs that you feel these need something, serve them with bottled Chinese duck sauce or just apricot jam. But do try them plain first; then you'll know what pork really tastes like. The only reason I don't have these as often as baked breast of lamb is that they're usually several times as expensive.

Pork Chops in Mustard Sauce

L'il Abner's relatives aren't the only ones to ever have a craving for pork chops. The Yokums couldn't possibly love them any more than I do, though I spread my food cravings around a lot more than they seem to. And I'm happy to have my pork chops in any of a number of ways: broiled, braised, baked in sour cream and so on. But since I've discovered pork chops in mustard sauce, I yearn for them just as much as any Yokum could for the fried version.

Treat yourself to a really large, top-quality center-cut pork chop. (It can't possibly cost you any more than a week's pay.) Trim off any large amount of excess fat; just leave a little around the edges.

Brown the chop thoroughly but very, very slowly in 1 tablespoon of butter; this should take at least half an hour and possibly more.

Put the chop on a warm plate or hot tray. Add 1 tablespoon of wine vinegar to the pan in which you cooked the chop. Stir it around to bring up the nice brown glaze on the bottom of the pan. Now stir in first ½ teaspoon of Dijon mustard, then ¼ cup of heavy cream, a pinch of dried thyme and salt and pepper. Simmer, stirring, for 3 to 4 minutes, then pour over the chop.

That's perfection in pork chops.

Fried Salt Pork with Cream Gravy

Fried salt pork with its traditional accompaniment of cream gravy has been warming farmers and plain people everywhere since colonial days. Warming them and giving them the strength to go out and move boulders, plow fields, pull out tree stumps. Perhaps you don't need quite that much strength, but try this dish anyway. Excess strength never did anyone any harm, and this is delicious food.

¼ pound salt pork	*1 or 2 tablespoons butter or lard*
Boiling water	*1 tablespoon flour for gravy*
Salt and pepper	*½ cup milk*
Flour or cornmeal for dredging	

Slice the salt pork ¼ inch thick. Pour boiling water over it, then drain. (This removes the excess salt.)

Dip the slices in salt-and-pepper-seasoned flour or cornmeal (I prefer the flour). Melt the butter or lard in a frying pan (a cast-iron skillet for me) and cook the salt pork slices slowly in it until both sides are golden brown. Remove them to a warm plate.

Pour off some of the fat in the skillet, leaving just about 2 tablespoons. Stir in the flour, then the milk, and continue stirring while cooking over a slow fire until the gravy has thickened. If it thickens too much, add more milk. Taste to see if it needs more salt and pepper.

Serves 1.

Serve your fried salt pork and its creamy-if-not-really-cream gravy on or with toast or mashed or boiled potatoes. Fried apples (page 238) seem a natural side dish with this, too. Don't worry about calories. If you're going to have a meal this fattening you might as well go all out.

Spaghetti alla Carbonara

When Billie Jean King had her big tennis match with Bobby Riggs in October 1973, we asked some people at the last minute to come drink, eat and watch the television coverage with us. *Spaghetti alla Carbonara* is what I served them, thinking it would be soothing to all, no matter which player they were rooting for —and easy for me to cook, as well. I made quite a lot of the *carbonara,* but I should have made more: our guests seemed to need a lot of soothing before the match. After the tennis, everyone rejoiced. It turned out they all—male and female alike— were pulling for Ms. King.

2 pieces bacon, diced
¾ cup ham, cut into small strips
2 tablespoons butter, softened
1 whole egg plus 1 yolk
½ cup heavy cream
¼ cup Parmesan or Romano
  cheese, freshly grated (plus extra to add at the table)

½ pound spaghetti
Salt and pepper
¼ teaspoon red pepper flakes
  (optional)

Cook the bacon briefly until it gives up some of its fat. Add the ham strips and cook for another minute or two, stirring, until they're both fairly brown and crisp. Remove from the fire.

Cream the butter until it's very soft.

Beat the egg and the yolk briefly, then add the heavy cream and the grated cheese. (I put them all in the blender and turn it on for just a moment or two.)

Cook the spaghetti in 3 or 4 quarts of salted water to which you've added a few drops of oil. If you have an attractive Dutch oven, use it for this process. While the spaghetti is cooking, reheat the bacon and ham and reblend the liquid mixture. After 10 to 12 minutes, drain the spaghetti (dumping it into a colander in the sink is the easiest way).

Put the spaghetti back into its pot. Stir in the butter, tossing the spaghetti like a salad. Turn the heat on very low. Toss in the bacon and ham with their fat; then the egg, cream and cheese combination. Add some salt and pepper and, if you want their pleasant bite, the red pepper flakes. Work fast, because while you want the eggs to be cooked, you don't want them *over*cooked. Taste to make sure there's enough salt.

If you've used a good-looking pot to cook this in, serve the *carbonara* right in that. Otherwise, transfer it quickly to a bowl that you've heated by rinsing with hot water, then drying.

This much *spaghetti alla carbonara* will serve two or three. For more or less, multiply or divide at will.

Mince, or Collop

Mince—sometimes known as collop—is as Scottish a food as there could be, except perhaps for oatmeal and shortbread. It sounds pretty awful, hamburger cooked in water, but it's elemental-tasting and marvelous. Why do you suppose that, as far as I know, only the Scots have thought of this simple way of cooking their minced beef? They seem to have a natural bent for the soothing in food, and no doubt that their *haggis* (liver and oatmeal and beef fat and such, cooked in a sheep's stomach) is the most soothing of all. I don't think I'll ever know, or at least I sincerely hope not.

½ pound chopped beef (chuck or round)
1 tablespoon butter
Salt and pepper

1 small onion, minced (optional)
1 small carrot, minced (optional)
¼ cup boiling water

Brown the ground meat in the butter in a small frying pan, cooking and stirring slowly, not allowing any lumps to form. Add the salt and pepper and, if you wish, the onion and carrot. (Add these only if you feel like mincing them and then eating them, or if you feel you need some vitamins. The dish is just as good one way or the other.) Add the water. Cover the pan. Simmer for half an hour, or until the meat is soft and the juice has almost disappeared. Stir several times during the cooking, to keep the meat from sticking, and add water if the mixture is getting very dry.

Mince, or collop (there seems to be some confusion over the name; it may depend on what part of Scotland you're from), is fine just by itself, but extra-fine served on top of mashed potatoes.

Carlynn's Chili con Carne

Chili will warm you inside and out and all the way down to your toes. This recipe is as unauthentic as you can get (tomato soup, indeed), but you can't find one that tastes better—at least to *gringos*. Carlynn Brook, whose recipe this is, is from Canada; so that may help explain why her chili sounds so north-of-the-border. But she's spent a lot of time in Mexico lately and still likes her chili made this way. I do, too.

1 large onion, chopped
1 green pepper, chopped
1 large stalk celery, chopped
½ pound ground beef, chuck or round
1 teaspoon butter
1 can tomato soup

1 soup can of water
1 can kidney beans
1½ teaspoons white vinegar
½ teaspoon chili powder
½ teaspoon Tabasco sauce
½ teaspoon salt

Brown the onion, green pepper, celery and ground beef in the butter. Add the tomato soup, water, kidney beans and vinegar. (And the white vinegar is important; the chili doesn't taste right without it, or with any other sort of vinegar.) Now add the chili powder, Tabasco and salt. Simmer until the sauce thickens—

and this is a long time, so settle down with something appropriate like tequila and just stir the mixture once in a while. Toward the end of the cooking, you may have to scrape the chili down from the sides of the pan now and then. Taste to see if there's enough chili powder, Tabasco and salt, and add more if needed.

Two things about the practicality of this chili. If you wait to make it until a time comes when you're cold enough to need it, you'll be well warmed up by the time it's ready to eat. So anticipate: make it ahead and keep it in the refrigerator or, for a longer haul, the freezer. The other point is that even a very hungry person in need of soothing warmth would have a little trouble eating all this, but there's no way of making a smaller amount—at least not without being very wasteful, using a half-can of this and a half-can of that. So refrigerate or freeze in two or more batches. Then you can half-freeze yourself to death more than once, or invite an icy friend in to share this warming repast.

Steak Tartare

New York is an amazing town. Many of its sandwich counters and hamburger places do a booming business delivering orders to offices. A hot dog and French fries here, a bacon, lettuce and tomato there; also salads, hot plates of various sorts and such surprising items as Chinese roast pork sandwiches, complete with duck sauce and hot mustard. And even steak tartare, presented in a rather elegant fashion, garnished with parsley, with the meat cold and the toast warm. On a day when you're working so hard you can't get out to lunch, this can give you a tremendous lift.

For steak tartare—or tartar steak, if you'd rather—you can be a purist and use scraped raw steak, or you can be more practical and use a good grade of chopped beef. You can mix everything together, as I've told you to below, or you can make a mound of the beef, place the egg yolk in a small depression you've made in the top, then put little piles of the other ingredients around the meat. This looks pretty at the beginning, but soon becomes a mess as you mix or fiddle around with it.

½ *pound chopped good-quality* *sirloin, round or chuck*	*Salt and pepper* *Worcestershire sauce (optional)*
2 *tablespoons minced onion*	*Anchovies (optional)*
1 *egg yolk*	2 *pieces buttered toast, halved*
1 *tablespoon capers*	

Mix the meat, onion, egg yolk, capers, salt and pepper together lightly. (Use more onion and capers if you want—these are starter amounts.) Add a little Worcestershire if you think the meat needs it; taste it first to find out. If you choose to use anchovies, it's better to drape them on the top of the finished product than to chop or mash them and mix them in now.

Form the meat into a mound on a plate. A little lettuce underneath would look nice, but certainly isn't necessary. Put the toast around the meat, provide yourself with a butter knife and sit down to a rather odd but delightful feast.

Steak tartare is also good to serve with drinks. In that case, provide small toast squares, buttered or dry.

As I said above, if you mix steak tartare at the table, it gets messy looking. However, there's something to be said for not mixing the meat at all (except for adding the yolk—I'd still do that in the kitchen). It can be fun to make each bite taste different, to think to yourself, "Hmm . . . I think I'll have nothing but capers and meat this time," or "Onions and anchovies and just a little meat should be good."

Hamburgers au Poivre

Sometimes when you're in a rotten mood it's because you're broke. Cultivate the thinking of Mike Todd, who is supposed to have said, "I've been broke many times, but I've never been poor." And learn to make do for the time being with reasonable substitutes for luxury foods. For *steak au poivre*, for instance, try hamburgers given the same treatment.

Use ⅓ to ½ pound of good ground beef (chuck or round) for each hamburger. Mix into the meat, for each pound: 1 egg, 2 tablespoons of milk, a tablespoon of lemon juice and a dash of Worcestershire or other meat sauce or ½ teaspoon of Bovril or Maggi. Form patties. Dredge heavily with lots of freshly ground black pepper and press it in. Let sit for at least half an hour.

Sear both sides in 1 tablespoon each of butter and oil in a hot skillet. Turn the heat down and cook, turning a time or two, until you reach the degree of doneness you want. Put patties on warm platter.

Remove the pan from the fire. Add 2 tablespoons of brandy. Swirl it around. Add 2 tablespoons of heavy cream. Cook, stirring, until the sauce thickens. Pour over the hamburgers. (Use rolls if you want, though I never do.)

If you're really broke omit the cream. If you're in *desperate* financial shape, leave the brandy out, too. Just serve the patties with some butter on each. It will still be *hamburgers au poivre*.

And see the next recipe for how to have almost-lamb chops when the budget screams for help.

Lamburgers

When lamb chops are too expensive to even dream about, console yourself with lamburgers. They taste remarkably like the best loin chops—just a little easier to chew. And ground lamb is always inexpensive, comparatively speaking.

> Use fairly lean ground lamb, if possible. Form into ⅓- to ½-pound patties. Wrap each in a strip of bacon; fasten with toothpicks.
>
> Pan broil like so: Brown each side in a fairly hot skillet. Then lower the heat and turn each patty up on edge so the bacon will cook. Prop them against the edge of the pan so they'll stay upright. Roll the patties along until the whole strip on each burger is cooked. At this point, the lamb will have reached just the right state of doneness.

Serve topped with the same bit of plain or chive butter you would use on a regular lamb chop (page 47). In a world where substitutes abound, this is one of the best ones.

Bolsagen Kofte

This Armenian supper is one of the very favorite dishes of all three of my children, even the ones who tend to be difficult about food. I don't mind it a bit myself, and my husband gobbles it down with the best of them. It's the *avgolemono*—egg and lemon—principle carried to full-meal heights, and it's fairly easy to cook and unbelievably easy to eat. A soother *par excellence.*

½ *pound ground lamb*
1 *small onion, minced*
½ *cup minced parsley*
¼ *cup raw rice*
½ *teaspoon dried basil or mint*
Salt
Pepper

3 *small eggs*
¼ *cup flour, more or less*
3½ *cups beef broth (make it*
 with bouillon cubes if you want
 or try chicken broth instead)
Juice of 1 lemon

Mix together the lamb, onion, parsley, rice, basil or mint, salt, pepper and 1 of the eggs. Form into small balls about the size of golf balls; roll in flour. Bring the broth to a full boil in a deep pot. Add the lamb balls one by one, so the broth never stops boiling. Cover and boil slowly for 20 minutes. Beat the remaining 2 eggs and the lemon juice very thoroughly (I do this in a blender); then add to them, while continuing to beat or blend, a couple of ladlesful of broth from the pot. Quickly stir this combination into the broth and meatballs. Serve at once, because the broth thickens too much if left to stand for more than a few minutes. However, it should have some body; if it doesn't, cook for a minute or two more. Needless to say, serve in soup plates or deep bowls, and don't bother to have anything else with it. This recipe makes enough to serve 1½ or 2 people. If you're hungry, you'll probably qualify as 1½, but *bolsagen kofte* is so good you really should share it with someone else. To serve 3 or 4, just double everything except the eggs: use 3 large ones instead of 3 small. In fact, if you only have large eggs on hand when making the amount given above, just beat or blend 2 of them, then use ⅓ in the meatballs and the rest in the broth.

Bolsagen kofte is soothing in more than one way. It has a strange, beneficial effect on the nervous system, to be sure. Also, though, the fact that ground lamb is usually one of the most inexpensive meats around has its own calming effect, at least on the person who does the shopping.

Sausage Pie

If you love sausage, here is the pie for you. The sausage meat is crumbled and crisp, the mashed potatoes smooth and bland and the bread crumbs somehow pull the whole thing together. . . . Very nice.

First, the mashed potatoes: Follow the directions on page 120 or use instant potatoes—the amount the package says will make 2 or 3 servings, but use more milk and butter than the directions call for. About double. Put the mashed potatoes into a pie plate so they form a rather thick crust.

Brown ½ pound of sausage meat, crumbling it as it cooks. Lift out with a slotted spoon and place in the mashed potato shell. (Actually, I'd use a whole pound of sausage, but I'm a *real* sausage lover.) Pour off all but about 1 tablespoon of sausage fat. Add to what's left in the pan a tablespoon or so of vegetable oil, and into this crumble finely 2 pieces of bread. Add a chopped scallion or some chives; then either just stir or cook gently until browned. This mixture goes on top of the sausage, and the "pie" goes into a 350° oven for 10 minutes, or until it's lightly browned.

If I'm serving this as a main dish, I like to have something sharp and cold with it—tomatoes and cucumbers in wine vinegar and herbs, for instance. But sausage pie's main function in this world is as a lunch or supper all in itself, where it's pleasantly soporific, if not absolutely stupefying.

Serves 2 or 3.

Hot Dogs in Barbecue Sauce

This is a great deal better than it sounds. It's delicious, once you get over the necessary mental hurdles, and a real soother when you want something hot, filling and down to earth.

5 or 6 hog dogs	*1 tablespoon prepared mustard*
2 tablespoons bacon fat	*½ tablespoon vinegar*
2 tablespoons minced onion	*½ teaspoon sugar*
⅓ cup catsup	*A good dash of salt*
1 tablespoon Worcestershire	*A pinch of chili powder (optional)*
sauce	*½ cup strong beef bouillon*

This sauce will handle up to ½ pound of hot dogs. ("Frankfurters," you say? Oh!) Make a deep gash lengthwise in each one. Start browning them in the bacon fat; after a couple of minutes, add the minced onion. When the hot dogs and onion are brown, mix together all the other ingredients and add them to the pan. Simmer for 20 minutes, uncovered, turning the hot dogs from time to time. The sauce should be thick at the end of the 20 minutes; if it's not, turn the heat up and boil the sauce down for a minute or two.

Serve with something you can put this good sauce onto. Mashed potatoes, *I* say, but you might prefer rice or toast or noodles.

This is a fine barbecue sauce for other purposes, too. You could simmer chopped meat in it for sloppy Joes, thin it down and use it to cook spareribs and . . . oh, all sorts of things. Serves 2 or 3.

Chicken Breasts Poached with Lemon

Hope Peek, my oldest, dearest, etc., friend, has a natural elegance. So it should have been no surprise that when I asked her for her ideas on soothing foods, the first thing she came up with was chicken breasts, "skinned and boned—you know, suprêmes—poached in chicken broth with a little lemon juice and grated lemon peel."

1 chicken breast (actually a half-breast), skinned and boned
1 cup chicken broth, as rich as possible (homemade or canned)
½ teaspoon lemon juice
⅛ teaspoon grated lemon rind
Salt and pepper

Combine the chicken breast, broth, lemon juice and lemon rind in a small pan. The chicken breast will probably be about half-covered. Simmer gently, covered, for 20 to 25 minutes, turning the chicken once or twice. Add salt and pepper. Serve on rice to one.

You should know, though, that this isn't at all the way Hopie told me the recipe. Like all good cooks, she gave no measurements. It was, "a little of this and a little of that." To be more exact, to serve two, she uses "a squirt" of lemon juice. At another time, she said, "Of course, to have it be *really* soothing, you add an egg yolk at the end, and then what you have is egg and lemon soup." (And we already have egg and lemon soup, *Avgolemono* —see page 27—as I told her.) What I'm sure she does—and it works for me—is to beat the egg yolk, add it to a dipperful (roughly ½ cup) of the broth, then quickly blend that into the dish. She flattered me by not giving any further directions.

To me, this is the height of simple, soothing elegance.

Chicken Steamed in Port

Agatha Starkey was the nurse for my children when they were small and I was working. She is a lovely woman from the island of Jamaica, and half-Chinese. She would cook for us occasionally—wild, marvelous half-Chinese, half-Jamaican dishes, full of ginger root and bamboo shoots.

Perhaps the most intriguing dish was one she cooked for Clark, my husband, the day he returned from the hospital after a bad case of pneumonia. Agatha said it it was the standard food among the Chinese of Jamaica for those who needed strength.

> To make it, she cut the meat of half a chicken (or it may have been just the chicken breasts) into bite-size pieces, put them into a bowl and poured on enough port wine to completely cover the pieces. Then she put the bowl in an improvised steamer and cooked it over low heat for 1 hour or a little longer. (The steamer: a large pot and a small trivet. An inch or so of water went into the pot, and the bowl of chicken and wine sat on the trivet. The pot was then tightly covered.) She served it to Clark in a small bowl, wine and all.

Fortunately, Agatha made a lot of the chicken steamed in port, because after one taste of it, I decided I needed some strengthening, too, and ate every bit as much as the patient.

Bread-and-Milk Chicken

One recent day I felt utterly jaded with food. I was hot, I was tired, I was discouraged: I was generally miserable. All I had available to cook was some chicken parts, and I knew I couldn't possibly bear to eat, let alone cook, any of the chicken dishes I could think of. Fried, cacciatore, all that sort of thing— just the thought of them made me slightly ill.

Then up from my subconscious, I guess, came a dim memory of something I'd had years ago; something so simple, so down-to-earth, so soothing, that I knew that was what I had to have.

I put the chicken parts into a small, very well-buttered casserole, just barely large enough to hold them. Then I tore up pieces of white bread, crusts and all, and stuffed them into every nook and cranny I could find; more torn-up bread went on top. I poured on enough milk to just cover everything and added a tablespoon of butter on top of it all.

The casserole baked at 350°, uncovered, until the top became slightly brown and a poke with a fork assured me that the chicken was tender.

By then, the milk had disappeared and the bread was unrecognizable: it had become just a lovely white stuffing sort of thing, full of the flavors of the butter and milk and the goodness that oozed out of the chicken as it baked. It was perfect for the way I felt, and so delicious that I plan to need this particular form of soothing quite often.

Brunswick Stew

The first time I tasted Brunswick Stew, I was in my late teens and temporarily in desperate need of something both soothing and sustaining. It was a Sunday night after a weekend that had included a college dance, driving 200 miles to another college on an insane impulse to see some friends and take them to breakfast (they were quite surprised), playing in a softball game and a general frenzy of activity. Fun—but when Sunday night came, all of us who had indulged in this manic activity were limp. We all ended up being served Brunswick Stew by a wonderful woman, Thyra Cahoon Noll, the mother of two of my friends. We just sat around and ate bowl after bowl of it, feeling perceptively better after each bite. Mrs. Noll understood teenagers, and since she was originally from the South (North Carolina) she really knew how to make Brunswick Stew. Here is her recipe, thanks to Edna Wenk, one of her daughters.

4-pound stewing chicken
4 quarts water
½ pound salt pork, cubed
1 pint corn kernels, canned, frozen or cut off the cob
1 pint lima beans
8 medium potatoes, peeled and cut in chunks

8 medium onions, cut up
2 tablespoons sugar
Salt and pepper
1 quart tomatoes, canned or fresh —peeled, seeded and chopped
¼ pound butter

Cook the chicken in the water until the meat falls from the bones; remove the bones. Add the salt pork to the chicken and broth. Bring to a boil. Add the corn, lima

beans, potatoes, onions, sugar and some salt and pepper. Cook slowly for 3 hours. Add the tomatoes and
butter and simmer for 1 hour more. Now Mrs. Noll's
recipe says to thicken slightly. Probably she mixed a
little of the broth with some flour, then stirred it into
the stew. But you could just boil it down quickly, instead.

Obviously you can't run up a little Brunswick Stew on a moment's notice. It's at least a 6-hour deal. But you could serve it
to guests some time and freeze what's left to have in time of
need. This recipe serves twelve, as you might guess from the
large amounts of everything.

Chicken Lobscouse

My daughter Candy was only about seven years old when she
invented Chicken Lobscouse. The regular Beef Lobscouse (page
39) was then (and still is) her idea of a proper dinner, and she
did (and does) put in frequent requests for it. One day she
wanted her Lobscouse quite badly, but I explained that we were
having chicken for dinner. "Well, why couldn't you make Lobscouse out of chicken?" she asked. Why not? I did, and it was
marvelous. Just as delicious, in its own way, as Beef Lobscouse,
and just as soothing.

To make it, follow the instructions on page 39 for Lobscouse,
simply substituting cut-up chicken for beef. The cooking time
will be somewhat shorter. Remove the chicken bones before serving.

Creamed Chicken and Ham

In the course of writing this book, I have come to realize that my father is quite an expert on mood food. There are times when, to suit (or palliate) a mood, it seems as though he absolutely *has* to have one food or another. Some of his specials are creamed chipped beef, crackers and milk, and chili (which you'll find, respectively, on pages 40, 235 and 55, though it's *canned* chili he usually eats, and he eats it with crackers on the side). I haven't heard him mention creamed chicken and ham for years, but his requests for it were a recurring obligato in my childhood. Now that I've reminded him of it, I probably should see him right away and make him a big batch of his old favorite.

Make a rich cream sauce: Melt 1½ tablespoons of butter. Blend in 1½ tablespoons of flour, then ½ cup of chicken broth and ¼ cup of heavy cream. Cook slowly, stirring, until sauce comes to a boil. Let it cook over the lowest possible heat for 5 minutes more; remove from heat. Add ½ cup of cooked chicken and ¼ cup of cooked ham, both of them diced or shredded. Add pepper and, if it's needed, salt, tasting carefully. Add a little more cream if you want a thinner sauce.

This will feed two. Serve in patty shells or on toast . . . or cornbread . . . or English muffins . . . or biscuits. But to make my father really happy, I'll have to serve it to him on waffles.

Red-Cooked Chinese Chicken

Sometimes when you crave Chinese food, you don't feel like going to all the effort that cooking it involves, or even like going to get it at a Chinese take-out place.

At these times, you can make such simple dishes as *congee* (page 9) or Chicken Steamed in Port (page 64), though these don't taste terribly Chinese, or this Red-Cooked Chinese Chicken. It's easy and it's good and it tastes (and is) *very* Chinese. "Red-cooked" just means cooked in soy sauce. This dish has enough soy to take care of the craving for salt that might be what made you yearn for Chinese food in the first place.

Chicken parts (for instance, 2 thighs or drumsticks—to serve 1)
½ cup soy sauce
1 cup water
1 tablespoon sherry
1 or 2 thin slices ginger root, fresh or canned (or substitute ¼ teaspoon ground ginger)

2 or 3 stalks of scallion, cut up
1 star anise, if available (if not, don't use a substitute)
1 tablespoon sugar

Combine all ingredients. Simmer for 45 minutes, turning occasionally if the sauce doesn't cover the chicken. Serve hot or cool, with the sauce as is or cooked down as much as you want for a more concentrated flavor.

This much sauce will cook enough chicken parts to serve one to three people. If you want to pamper the soy-cravings of a larger group, use a whole stewing chicken and double the ingredients for the sauce. Simmer for 1½ hours, turning and basting from time to time.

Chicken à la King

The people whose mood is brightened by Chicken à la King must have had happy times in the past at luncheons, charity balls and birthday parties, since—always in patty shells and usually accompanied by green peas—it has been the staple food for such functions for generations.

> Follow the instructions for Creamed Chicken and Ham on page 68, but omit the ham. Briefly and gently sauté ¼ cup of sliced mushrooms and 2 tablespoons each of diced green pepper and pimiento in 2 tablespoons of butter. Add this mixture to the creamed chicken along with 1 tablespoon of dry sherry.

Serve this (in larger quantities, of course) for your next luncheon, charity ball or birthday party. But please don't invite me, thank you just the same. I've had enough Chicken à la King in the past to last me all the rest of my days.

Cold Lobster with Mayonnaise

A few years ago I somehow found myself having dinner on election day all by myself in a room at the Plaza Hotel in New York. It was for complicated but valid reasons: my husband was supervising an election-results broadcast, I was to join him *after dinner* (that was put to me rather emphatically) and then we were to spend the night in town.

Valid reasons or no, I was a little sad about eating alone. So in a spirit of slight rebellion I picked up the room-service menu and looked for something to order. Surely it was just coincidence that made me choose the most expensive thing on the menu. It was served to me as though I were a reigning princess, and my feelings were considerably salved by indulging in so much luxury.

Ideally, or so I think, you should call a sympathetic fish man early in the day and ask him to boil and chill a small—no bigger than 1½ pounds—lobster for you. While he's at it, he might as well split and clean it for you, too. If you don't mind slaughter in your kitchen, though, cook the beast yourself.

Bring a large pot of salted water to a full, rolling boil. Put the lobster in, head first. (Don't worry about being pinched by a claw; surely your lobster man has pegged them. Otherwise, grab it just behind the head.) Cover the pot tightly and boil for 20 minutes.

Now you will have the fun of cleaning the lobster. It's not too bad. Put it on its back on a cutting board or platter. You'll see a line running down the middle; cut this open with a scissors or sharp knife. Then crack the shell open and remove the dark vein and the hard sac under the head. The green and red substances you see are edible. Crack the claws quickly (use lobster-cracking gadgets or a hammer or whatever you have) so any water in them can drain out. Chill thoroughly.

Serve with mayonnaise, a homemade one (you'll have to see some other cookbook—maybe my own *Impromptu Cooking*, Atheneum, 1973) or one you've devised by taking ¼ cup of a good commercial brand such as Hellman's and adding to it the juice of ¼ lemon and 2 or 3 tablespoons of light olive oil.

If you don't want this much luxury—or expense—even cold boiled frozen lobster tails are very soothing when served with a good mayonnaise. Use your best china; that always helps.

Oyster Loaf

An oyster loaf has just *got* to be a good mood-changer, because in at least two major American cities, far apart from each other, there's a tradition that this is the very thing for an out-too-late husband to take home to mollify his wife. The cities: San Francisco and New Orleans. Here is a recipe to serve one.

For each "loaf," use a crusty roll, the kind you might use for a hero (sub, grinder, etc.). Cut it in two lengthwise, making the cut near the top of the loaf. Hollow out the insides; remove most of the soft bread. Save these crumbs—you may or may not need them. Brush the shell of the loaf amply with melted butter. Bake at 375° until it's a light golden brown.

Now fry the oysters, 6 or 7 frying-size ones. Some authorities say to bread them; some say not to. Since I have never been a wife in need of mollification in either old San Francisco or New Orleans, I really don't know the "proper" way. But in this case I tend toward breading. So dip the oysters first in an egg that has been beaten with 1 tablespoon of oyster liquor, then in fine, dry crumbs of bread or crackers. Sauté in 2 or 3 tablespoons of butter for about 3 minutes, or until the edges curl. If you're against breading, just sauté the naked oysters in butter.

Put the fried oysters in the bread case. Sprinkle on some salt and pepper to taste. Now, if your oysters are small and they're rattling around in the case, fill in the larger chinks with the soft bread you've saved. Over the oysters (and especially over the bread, if you're using it), sprinkle a mixture of melted butter and heavy cream, about 1 tablespoon of each. But save 1 or 2 teaspoons of the mixture to brush on the top of the loaf. Bake at 375° for 10 minutes, or until good and hot.

After tasting these, I think it's possible that some San Francisco and New Orleans wives encouraged their husbands to stay out late just so they'd get such oyster loaves.

The use of crusty rolls, by the way, is mine. The traditional oyster loaf is made in a full-size loaf, preferably of French bread. That's a lot of food—the errant husbands must have helped with the eating of it.

Scalloped Oysters

Scalloped oysters take me back to happy Thanksgivings with my mother, when she would serve turkey, country ham *and* scalloped oysters, not to mention fruit cocktail, soup, mashed potatoes, mashed turnips, green beans with almonds, stuffing, celery and olives, mixed nuts, cranberry sauce, pumpkin pie, mince pie, apple pie, ice cream and cheese. And, of course, cocktails, hors d'oeuvres, wine, coffee and brandy. We were a little full after these meals.

For me, nowadays (and for Mother most of the time, except for Thanksgivings in those days), scalloped oysters make a full meal. Maybe with a little green salad on the side, at the most. Here's how our family likes them—plain, bland and oystery.

1 cup (½ pint) oysters
¼ cup heavy cream
¾ cup saltine crumbs (or substi-
    tute dry bread crumbs for all
    or part)
4 tablespoons butter, melted

Salt and pepper
1 to 2 tablespoons unmelted but-
    ter
Paprika

Drain the oysters, reserving the liquor and combining it with the cream. Combine the crumbs and the melted butter with some salt and pepper. Now start assembling in a small, well-buttered baking dish: a layer of ⅓ of the crumb-butter mixture; a layer of ½ of the oyster; another layer of ⅓ of the crumbs; the rest of the oysters; then the rest of the crumbs. On top of each layer of oysters, sprinkle ½ of the cream–oyster liquor combination. When this is all assembled, dot the top with the unmelted butter and sprinkle on just a little paprika.

Bake at 400° for 20 minutes. Don't overbake or bake ahead and keep warm, lest the oysters lose their freshness and pizzazz, but it's all right to do the assembling 1 or 2 hours before baking.

Serves 2.

Scalloped oysters are a sort of solid oyster stew, excellent for times when you want pure oyster flavor but don't want soup. They are really, really good.

Barbara's Crab Cakes

People who live around Chesapeake Bay truly love their crab cakes, and there are dozens of recipes for them. This one is from a recipe file of my mother's. Mother used to get back-fin crab meat from a local crab man on the Eastern Shore of Maryland, make up a batch of crab cakes, wrap each one in foil and freeze them. Whenever she felt like it, she had a crab cake all set to cook. This was, as I recall, every day for lunch for a while. I'm allergic to crab, so I don't know, but I'm told that crab cakes are tremendously satisfying and happy-making.

1 pound crab meat
4 tablespoons butter, melted
2 tablespoons chopped parsley
1 teaspoon lemon juice
⅛ teaspoon cayenne pepper
¼ teaspoon sugar

2 slices white bread, cubed, or an equivalent amount of crushed saltines (I gather the saltines are better than the bread)
About ⅓ cup mayonnaise, just enough to bind everything together

Mix all the ingredients together, adding the mayonnaise last. You'll want to use just enough of it to make a moist, soft mixture with enough body so it can be shaped into cakes.

Form into 8 to 10 crab cakes. Cook in a little melted butter until they are a golden brown. (Dredge the cakes with flour or fine bread crumbs first if you want a crisper crust.)

Who was Barbara? I'm not sure—possibly Mother's hairdresser. At any rate, she might have trouble recognizing her recipe, since it's clear from the file card that mother made rather extensive changes, such as adding the lemon juice, cayenne and sugar and deleting the mustard that was in Barbara's version.

Don't be haughty at the thought of using mayonnaise in food to be cooked. It turns up now and then in some of the finest French cooking. The ingredients that make up mayonnaise—egg, oil, vinegar or lemon juice, salt and pepper—add good flavor, and the texture adds creaminess.

Baked Clams

Clam dishes, like those that feature oysters, *all* seem soothing to me. For one thing, there's just nothing easier to eat. But perhaps it's mostly the high dosage of good, natural sea minerals they hold. You can get a real craving for clams; so if you believe that what you crave is what you need (or if you just like to indulge your cravings), you'd better keep a can of minced clams on hand.

1 whole clove garlic
4-inch piece celery, minced
1 small onion, minced
1 tablespoon butter or oil, or
half-and-half of each
1 small can (7- or 8-ounce)
minced clams, juice and all

¼ cup grated Parmesan cheese
1 slice white bread, crumbed
¼ teaspoon oregano
1 tablespoon white wine
1 or 2 strips bacon

Sauté the whole garlic clove, the celery and onion gently in the butter and/or oil for a minute or two. Add the clams, complete with their juice, then the cheese and bread crumbs. (You may need slightly more or less of the bread crumbs—you want only enough to bind the mixture together.) Add the oregano and wine. Remove the garlic. (Or press the garlic at the beginning—if you're wild about garlic.)

Put this mixture into 2 large scallop shells, if you have them, or into small ramekins or clam shells. Top with the bacon—a half-strip per large shell, but a whole strip, cut in two, if it's skimpy bacon (and everything, led by candy bars, does keep getting skimpier). If it's very strong-tasting bacon, use just a little. I almost ruined our baked clams once by overpowering them with some of the lovely, cob-smoked bacon we get from Vermont.

Broil until the bacon is brown.

If baked clams can be classic, these are classic baked clams. A perfectly respectable addition would be 1 or 2 tablespoons of minced green pepper. Also, maybe, a chopped pimiento, or some minced mushrooms. But soothing food should be simple, so I suggest you keep these basic. You might even want to leave out the celery or the wine.

If you have real, honest-to-goodness fresh clams, use an equivalent amount—roughly 1 cup of clams and their juice—and chop them. The baking will cook them enough.

Serves 2 as a main course; 4 to 6 as an appetizer, depending on the size of your shells.

Steamed Clams

All my adult life I've dreamed of finding a place where you could go in shorts and bare feet or sneakers, sit overlooking the water and eat steamed clams and drink martinis. In my vision, this place is rather rustic, made of weathered boards that may have had an earlier life as barn siding. I think it's a porch we sit on with our clams and martinis. If I don't eventually find this place, I may have to create it myself. In the meantime, I can console myself with steamed clams at home, made this way.

Buy clams from a good fish man. Tell him you want them for steaming. "How many?" is a tricky question. If they're to be your whole meal (give or take a little corn-on-the-cob, perhaps), you'll need at least 1 quart per person.

At home, scrub them well, then put them in a big pot with just a little water, 2 or 3 tablespoons for each quart of clams. Cover tightly. Steam until all the clams are open, about 10 minutes.

To eat them, there's a ritual. Put the clams (it's a nice touch to wrap them in a large cloth napkin) in a big bowl or soup plate in front of each person. Give each diner a bowl of melted butter and a cup of the clam broth from the steaming pot. Provide another big bowl for the empty shells. To eat: pick a clam up by the neck; that's the part that sticks out like a handle. Dip it in the broth (which will remove any possible sand), then in the melted butter. Then pop it into your mouth and bite off all but the neck, which you discard. (I do, anyway, but it's perfectly edible.) When all the clams are eaten, pour the butter into the broth and drink this salubrious combination, all but the last ½ inch or so in the cup, which may be sandy.

The martinis to go with the clams are described in detail on page 220. Beer's good with clams, too, as is white wine, but you don't really need anything alcoholic to add to your enjoyment of these slippery delights. They're sufficient unto themselves.

Broiled Shad Roe

Shad roe is one of the few foods left that is truly seasonal. Our great-grandparents had to wait until the right time of year for lettuce, strawberries, peaches, fresh pork and so many other things, and probably appreciated them all the more for it. About all we have to wait for now is shad roe—you can't have it until the shad are running in the spring. (If you're wise in country lore, you can tell when this time comes because the shad bush will bloom. Or, anyway, that's what country people in the East will tell you.)

> Dip a pair of shad roe, split, into melted butter. Place on an oiled rack and broil about 4 inches from the flame for 6 minutes on the first side, 4 on the other. Baste with more melted butter as they cook. When done, season with salt and pepper and put a piece of butter on top—perhaps the chive butter suggested on page 47 for lamb chops, or some other herb butter. Garnish with crisp bacon.
>   Serves 2.

Because of my silly ideas about fish, I haven't tried shad roe, but this spring I think I will. People get so excited about it. Also, I like its simplicity, and it certainly does *look* good. So I may join the ranks of those whose spring isn't complete without shad roe. It seems to do for them what sulfur and molasses did for their ancestors. Why not me, too?

Barbara's Filet of Sole

A different Barbara from the crab-cake lady. This one's my friend Barbara Otto, and she came to my rescue when she learned that I, the fish-disliker, wanted to hear about fish recipes that some people consider soothing. This one sounds so elegant and generally smooth and delightful that I'll probably try it myself—but with chicken breasts, not sole. It's out of the ordinary, too. The green grapes would make it a sort of sole Véronique, but the tomatoes make it something else again.

Barbara's recipe was for four, and her sauce would be hard

to make in smaller quantities, so try this when there are three other people you feel could use some calming elegance.

4 filets of sole	*3 tablespoons butter*
½ cup white wine	*2 tablespoons heavy cream*
2 tablespoons sherry	*½ cup small seedless green*
Salt and pepper	*grapes*
3 egg yolks, beaten	*2 tomatoes, peeled, seeded and*
1 teaspoon tarragon vinegar	*cut into julienne strips*

If the filets need skinning and boning, take care of this; then wash and dry them if they seem to need it. Put the filets into a buttered baking dish. Pour on the white wine and sherry, combined; sprinkle on a little salt and pepper and bake at 300° for 20 minutes.

Remove the filets to a warm platter while you quickly prepare the sauce. Boil down the liquid remaining in the baking dish until only 3 or 4 tablespoons are left. Add this to the egg yolks, vinegar, butter and cream, which you've put in the top of a double boiler. Cook over boiling water, stirring all the while, until the sauce thickens. Taste to see if it needs more salt and pepper. Gently stir in the grapes and tomatoes. Pour onto the filets and serve immediately, accompanied by rice and a simple green salad, to four.

Good grief but that sounds marvelous!

EGGS AND CHEESE

EATING MOST OF THESE egg and cheese dishes produces an effect not too unlike curling up under a down comforter on a cold night. Warming, but even more to the soul than to the body. (That's a satin-covered down comforter, of course.)

But these recipes are multi-purpose. Lots of protein for energy. Occasional elegance for times when that's what you need. Lightness. Heartiness. For lunches, suppers, snacks. Look in the special Mood Index (page 241) for the sort of thing you need right-this-very-moment.

Most of these dishes can be made quickly and with ingredients you're apt to have on hand. One cheese dish that fits all these requirements you won't find here: the cheese sandwich. It's under Bread and Sandwiches.

Very Warm Shirred Eggs

A warmer-upper and a body and soul-soother. This came in handy recently after a winter indoor tennis game that ended at eight o'clock on a cold night. In a situation like that, you're all confused. You're warm from the tennis but chilled from coming home in the frigid air. You're tired, too, but not too tired to eat. This is the very thing.

1 tablespoon butter	*2 eggs*
⅓ cup heavy cream	*2 tablespoons grated Gruyère,*
2 tablespoons canned taco sauce	*Swiss or Parmesan cheese*
Tabasco sauce, if desired	*Salt and pepper, if desired*

Use the butter to generously grease a small ramekin or baking dish of some sort. Add the cream and the taco sauce and (or possibly *or*) enough Tabasco or other Louisiana hot sauce to make the sauce have the amount of piquancy you like. (Or if you'd rather, use a peeled green chili from a can and give it a quick whirl in the blender with the cream.) Onto this, carefully break the eggs. Top with the grated cheese. Bake at 375° for 8 to 10 minutes, or until the eggs are set and the cheese is beginning to brown. Sprinkle with a little salt and pepper, if desired.

Serves 1.

Eat this right out of the ramekin. If you have the strength left, you might like to accompany it with a large amount of crisp bacon. Nine slices didn't seem too much the other night after tennis. Perhaps exercise makes you crave protein?

Baked Eggs

A tradition in our house, this is the hot dish most requested when we're all exhausted for one reason or another; it's the easiest to make and the easiest to eat. No matter what meal the baked eggs are served for—breakfast, lunch, dinner or late-night supper—the most we ever have with them is biscuits, butter and jelly. Salad or vegetables just wouldn't do.

Here's what appears on my "Baked Eggs" file card. My current comments are in parentheses.

> Melt *lots* of butter in an ovenproof pan. (I really mean fireproof; what I use is a porcelain-over-cast-iron skillet. And by *lots* of butter, I mean 1 or 2 teaspoons per egg). Break in eggs. (Three per person, if they're hungry persons.) Almost cover with milk or cream. (So just the very tips of the yolks show. And it's usually milk I use. As a matter of fact, most of the time I *completely* cover the eggs with the milk.) Bake until the milk makes a sauce; add more milk if necessary. (The milk or cream actually does become a thick, clotted sauce.) Add salt and pepper (just sprinkle them on, of course) and serve.

I wasn't very specific on my file card about the temperature to use for the baking. That's because it doesn't matter: cook them at 300° if you're in no hurry, 350° if you're anxious to eat.

Chinese Steamed Eggs

These steamed eggs probably won't seem especially Chinese to you, except for the soy or oyster sauce that's added at the end. They are, though, much more authentically Chinese than Chop Suey, Fu Manchu or Charlie Chan. They're a sort of main-dish custard and extremely calming.

2 eggs

½ teaspoon sugar

Large pinch of salt

Small pinch of pepper

¾ cup chicken broth or water

2 teaspoons dry sherry, dry vermouth or rice wine

1 scallion, minced (optional)

1 to 2 teaspoons soy sauce or oyster sauce

The main trick to making these eggs is to keep as much air out of the mixture as possible in order to have the finished product smooth and unseparated. Thus, many books will tell you to boil the broth or water for several minutes, then let it cool slightly; also, to beat the eggs very, very lightly. I've found, though, that it's perfectly all right to use liquid that has merely come to a boil, then cooled a bit, and that a quick flick in the blender for the eggs does no harm. After all, you do have to beat the eggs somehow for long enough to make them smooth. So place the eggs in a blender container. Add the sugar, salt and pepper and turn the blender on (at low-to-medium speed if you have that sort of blender) for a few moments, just until the eggs are mixed enough so no transparent streaks of white show. Slowly stir in the broth or water, the sherry and the scallion, if you're using it. Pour into a small bowl. Put the bowl in a steamer of some sort (see page 64 for some clues on this), cover and cook over low heat until a table knife stuck into the custard comes out more or less clean. (With my particular steaming arrangement and my personal idea of "low" heat, this takes 8 or 9 minutes.) Pour on a teaspoon or more of soy or oyster sauce and eat the eggs right from their bowl.

Serves 1.

If you don't feel up to scallions, just don't use them. Also the soy sauce and pepper. For that matter, *add* anything that seems suitable to you—bits of cooked meat, slivered celery and so on.

Scrambled Eggs

If an egg is scrambled slowly, it will be soft, delicate and small-curd, also calming, soothing and comforting. If an egg is scrambled fast, over a rather high flame, it is only for the strong of stomach and of soul.

With that in mind, here's how to scramble an egg. Or, rather, two eggs—one scrambled egg never got anyone anywhere.

Beat 2 eggs with 1 teaspoon or so of liquid, usually milk or water. (I use a blender and turn it on very briefly, but that's awfully unorthodox.) Melt about 1½ tablespoons butter in a 6- or 7-inch frying pan. Add the beaten eggs and cook slowly, stirring all the while, until small curds begin to form. Remove from the heat and stir for a minute or two more, until the eggs are set but not dry. Season with salt and pepper. Serve at once. Another approach: do the cooking in the top part of a double boiler over simmering water, stirring only occasionally. This is easier, but it takes longer.

Serves 1.

These are perfect scrambled eggs, and exactly what you might want when your mood calls for just about the plainest possible food.

Variations on the Theme of Scrambled Eggs

When you feel up to a little more pizzazz than plain scrambled eggs (the previous recipe), a good move onward is to add some cheese. Just two or three tablespoons of any sort of cheese, grated or minced, added to the eggs at the start of cooking. (Try Cheddar, Parmesan, Roquefort, Gruyère, Camembert or cottage cheese.) By the time the eggs are cooked, the cheese will be melted.

To this you might want to add:

2 or 3 slices bacon, crisp and crumbled
A dash of paprika
1 peeled green chili, minced

A pinch of basil, thyme or tarragon
A tiny pinch of dry mustard

Try any of these, or whatever combination pops into your mind, or whatever you have on hand. Anything you might add to yogurt (see page 228) would work out well, even fruit, though it would be best to add that at the end of the cooking.

Hootsla

Half the fun of writing this book has been going through old family recipe files and notebooks. This morning I turned up Hootsla, something I haven't thought about for twenty years, (how could I have gone twenty years without Hootsla?) and realized that not only was it perfect for this book, but also that it was just exactly what I wanted for lunch.

Something puzzled me, though. The recipe card indicated that this was our own recipe (and it was written in my own handwriting, so I couldn't blame anyone else), but I was pretty sure I knew where to find something of the same name in a book on Pennsylvania Dutch cooking. I looked it up: *Hootsla,* sure enough, but far different from "our" version. So ours probably shouldn't be called Hootsla at all, but who could resist a name like that? Who could resist Hootsla itself, for that matter?

2 tablespoons butter
2 slices bread, cubed (stale bread is best)
1 tablespoon onion or scallion, minced

2 eggs, beaten with a tablespoon of milk or water
Salt and pepper to taste

Melt the butter in a small frying pan. Add the bread and onion and cook until they're just starting to brown. Add the eggs and stir for a moment; remove from the fire almost immediately, as soon as the eggs look set. Season to taste with salt and pepper.

If you have your Hootsla for breakfast, you'll probably want to omit the onion. (Or at least that's the way I feel about it.) The dish will be fine without it, though you might want to substitute bacon, partially cooked beforehand. For a light snack, cut all the ingredients except the butter in half.

Eggs Poached in Cream

Don't turn away just because you either don't like poached eggs or find them hard to make. These are the softest, smoothest, most sumptuous eggs you ever encountered, and while they are legitimately entitled to be called poached, there's none of that horrid shredding and bouncing around in the water that for many turns egg-poaching time into the torture hour. These eggs should tempt anyone to eat, no matter how terrible they feel.

1 tablespoon butter   *2 tablespoons heavy cream*
2 eggs   *Salt and white pepper to taste*

Use the full tablespoon to generously butter a small ramekin, baking dish or custard cup. Break the eggs carefully into the dish, then top with cream. Place the dish in a frying pan and add boiling water to the pan just up to the level of the cream in the dish. Cover the pan and cook with the water barely simmering until the whites of the eggs are set, about 6 minutes, but check to be sure. Sprinkle with salt and, if you feel up to anything even slightly spicy, the white pepper. Some buttered toast served with this would give you the old feeling of poached-eggs-on-toast—if you feel that's necessary.

Serves 1.

There's only one group of people who should not have poached eggs in cream: those with cholesterol problems.

A General Note on Various Quiches

In one of my many misguided (or at least ineffectual) attempts to lose weight, it occurred to me to make a *quiche* with no pastry. I just put whatever it was I was using into a pie pan and baked it. It was just fine—perhaps not *quite* as good as a regular *quiche,* particularly one in a crust of *pâte brisée* or flaky pastry (see page 231) but so much better than no *quiche* at all. Then about a week later, I went to a European *quiche*-fondue-etc. restaurant and ordered one of their "special" *quiches*. It came, and . . . **oops,** no crust! Special, indeed!

So with these *quiches* or any others, cook in a crust or not, depending on the time and energy available and whether or not you want to eliminate a lot of calories. If you use a crust, you can cook it in your fancy *quiche* pan, a flan ring or a pie pan. Without a crust, better stick to the pie pan, lest the custard ooze all over the floor of your oven.

One other note: I've made all these *quiches* in the proportions considered suitable to serve two to four as a main dish because, especially in a crust, they're hard recipes to cut in half. So save some for tomorrow, or give eating it all a really good try. I know you can do it!

Use any standard *quiche* recipe—or try these two unusual ones.

Cheshire Quiche

What comes to mind when you hear *Cheshire?* Cats? Smiles? Cheese? You might also give a thought to this very un-French *quiche,* based on English Cheshire pie.

Cooked pork, cubed	*Crust, if desired (see page 231)*
One apple, peeled and sliced	*2 eggs*
One medium onion, thinly sliced	*½ cup cream*
1 or 2 tablespoons butter	*½ cup milk (or use all milk, but*
A hefty pinch of powdered sage	*in that case make the total a*
Salt and pepper	*little less than 1 cup)*
1 tablespoon brown sugar (op-	
tional)	

"How much pork?" you ask. A little. Cook it, the apple and the onion in the butter for just a few minutes, until the apple no longer looks raw. Season to taste with the sage, salt and pepper and, if you think you'd like it, the brown sugar. Or use a little less brown sugar, or a little more. Poultry seasoning, perhaps, instead of sage. A bit of spice, if you want. They'd all be within the tradition, if that matters to you.

Put into a crust or just into a pie pan. Beat the eggs, cream and/or milk (try a blender). Pour on top of the pork mixture. Bake at 375° for about half an hour, or until the top is light brown.

Serves 2 to 4.

Go on, be brave—try the brown sugar in this, at least a little. It's half the charm of this aberrant *quiche.*

Cottage Quiche

Cottage *quiche* is one of the simpler, quicker-to-assemble *quiches.* You can put it together in about four minutes. If you omit the scallions, you can do it in one minute or less. It's no problem whatsoever to eat, either.

If scallions or shallots don't reach you at the moment, omit them. Perhaps substitute chopped pimiento, which would look pretty, or minced ripe olive.

2 tablespoons scallions or shallots, minced
3 tablespoons butter
3 cups cottage cheese, preferably creamed-style

3 tablespoons sour cream
½ teaspoon sugar
2 eggs, unbeaten
1 pie shell, unbaked (optional— see page 231)

Cook the scallions or shallots in the butter for 2 or 3 minutes. Stir in, one at a time, the cottage cheese, sour cream, sugar and eggs. Pour into the pie shell or a buttered ovenproof dish. Bake at 300° for 40 to 50 min-

utes, or until the *quiche* is puffed and the top looks set.
Serves 2 to 4.

If you're eating alone, try making a half-recipe of this, omitting the pie shell. Serve it with a *lot* of crisp bacon—indulge yourself. What a meal!

Fried Swiss Cheese

A wacky recipe, and a good one. It's related, I suppose, to the Swiss *raclette,* a fascinating dish in which a hunk of cheese is slowly melted by the fireside, and then is scooped out and put onto a baked or boiled potato. This is a little crisper, a little stranger, and a lot easier to do, particularly if you don't have a roaring fire going in your fireplace at the moment.

*¼ pound Swiss cheese at room
  temperature*
Flour for dredging

3 tablespoons butter
1 or 2 pieces buttered toast
Freshly ground black pepper

Cut the cheese into slices ¼ of an inch thick, then cut each slice into squares, rectangles, triangles or whatever strikes your fancy. The longest side of each piece should be about 1½ inches. Dip the pieces of cheese in flour; then fry them in butter that you have brought to the sizzling point. Turn them once or twice until they're golden brown. Place on the buttered toast and sprinkle with pepper. (This is one of the times when using freshly ground black pepper makes a large difference.)

Having the cheese at room temperature is vitally important; otherwise the flour won't stay on the cheese and the cheese won't hold its shape and what you end up with is a panful of run-together cheese with crisp edges—though that's pretty good, too.

Greek Baked Cheese

You probably won't be able to find this in a Greek cookbook; at least, I've never been able to. It may be a secret, or perhaps seems too simple to put down in writing. I think it's the former, because I ordered baked cheese in a Greek restaurant once, then asked the waiter what was in it. "Cheese," he said, smiling charmingly, "just cheese." "Nothing else?" I asked, trying to look knowing. "No, no, just cheese. Nothing else." And all the while, not only was there a lemony flavor to the dish, there was a lemon pit sitting right on top of the cheese. Ha! I've heard of restaurants holding back one ingredient when they give you a recipe, but it seems hardly fair at all when there are only two ingredients in the whole dish anyway.

Feta, the Greek cheese available in this country in glass jars, is the authentic cheese to use here, but I've found that good results come from any semi-hard cheese. Cheddar's fine, for instance, but best of all is Monterey Jack, particularly the kind sold in half-pound sticks.

Baked cheese is, I think, a marvelous dish to know about. It's quick, simple, delicious, and talk about soothing . . .

Use about ¼ pound semi-hard cheese. Slice this about ¼ of an inch thick (the shape and size of the slices don't matter, really, because they're going to melt together, anyway). Put into a well-butterd baking dish, sprinkle on 2 teaspoons of lemon juice and bake at 350° for 10 minutes, or until the cheese is melted and starting to brown.

Serves 1.

The result is a dish full of melted cheese, crisp at the edges and in spots on top, just slightly tart, soft and scrumptious. Depending on the cheese you use, there may be a good bit of a clear liquid floating around in the dish. Don't worry: it's just as good as the solid part of the cheese. Eat it, but you'd better use a spoon.

Spinach and Cheese Fondue

An *American* fondue, bearing absolutely no resemblance to the Swiss fondue except that both contain cheese. The original version of this was in a now-defunct magazine, *The Woman's Home Companion*. (It wasn't as turn-of-the-century as that name sounds. I think the magazine folded in the fifties, the *nineteen-*fifties.)

It's just a variation, jazzed up with spinach, of the egg, bread and cheese puddings that turn up in so many regional American cookbooks. Without the greenery, it's still a good and soothing meal. You can even leave out the onion. The French, incidentally, make something similar and sometimes come right out and call it a cheese soufflé. It is, too—sort of.

7 slices bread	*1 tablespoon lemon juice*
Butter	*A dash of ground cayenne pepper*
1 package spinach, thawed and	*or Tabasco sauce*
drained	*Salt and pepper*
2 tablespoons minced onion	*3 eggs*
1 cup grated Cheddar cheese	*1½ cups milk*

Remove the crusts from the bread. Butter lightly. Put 4 of the slices in the bottom of a large round baking dish or skillet. Cut the other 3 slices into 3 strips each; set aside.

Mix the spinach, onion, cheese, lemon juice, cayenne or Tabasco and salt and pepper; set aside.

Blend the eggs with the milk. Pour ½ cup of this onto the pieces of bread in the baking dish. Next, spread the spinach-cheese mixture over this. Now put on the reserved bread strips as though they were the spokes in a wheel. Pour on the rest of the egg-milk mixture. Let the dish sit for at least half an hour, then bake at 350° for 50 to 60 minutes.

This will serve 3 to 4 people. To serve 1½ to 2, cut everything in half as best you're able.

It's a *pretty* dish. The bread strip "spokes" puff up and brown and the spinach and cheese mixture glistens between them. It takes a little effort to make (not too much, though), but none at all to eat.

Welsh Rabbit

I think I'll be one of the few cookbook writers not to write a treatise on rabbit vs. rarebit, and to just let you call it whatever comes readily off your tongue. Whatever you call it, there are moods that won't be satisfied with anything else.

First, how to cook it. Then a few of the good ways to serve it.

1 tablespoon butter
½ pound Cheddar cheese,
  minced or grated
½ cup beer

¼ teaspoon dry mustard
A dash of Worcestershire sauce
A pinch of paprika

Melt the butter in the top of a double boiler or chafing dish. Add the cheese, then—bit by bit—the beer, stirring all the while. Add the seasonings. Keep stirring until the mixture is smooth, removing the pan from the hot water toward the end.

Serves 2 amply.

Serve on toast, crackers, English muffins or whatever you have in the bread line. Garnish with crisp bacon or fried, thin-sliced ham and wedges of tomato. Maybe also (or instead) with slices of avocado or radish.

Or broil some slices of tomato and onion (baste them with butter or oil as they cook) and serve the rabbit on them.

Or serve on a poached egg, perhaps with a base of toast or English muffins and bacon or ham—a kinda-sorta Eggs Benedict, with cheese sauce instead of hollandaise.

Or serve on hamburgers. Or spinach soufflé (page 129)—or on anything else that pops into your mind.

Rink Tum Diddy

For when you feel cheese-prone (not cheesy, necessarily), but don't quite want the purity and sharpness of a real Welsh rabbit-rarebit. This is honest-to-the-good-earth Americana. I've heard about it from several people and made it myself a time or two. It's good. Here's how my mother wrote it down in her first cooking notebook. (Can't say I remember her ever making it, though. She went in more for the real Welsh thing by the time I was old enough to notice.)

"Melt ½ pound American cheese. Add a few grains cayenne and 1 can tomato soup. Serve on toasted crackers."

Serves 2.

Other people have told me to use Cheddar cheese instead of American, add ½ can milk, cook it all in a double boiler, serve it on buttered toast. You can use it for any purpose real Welsh rabbit serves (take a look at the preceding recipe).

Real Swiss Cheese Fondue

Here's what Spring Brothers, manufacturers and importers of beautiful fondue equipment, have to say about the mood for cheese fondue: "It's cool outside but cozy in the home. Slowly it's getting dark and people are gathering around the table. What could suit this gathering better than a delicious Cheese Fondue."

They're right. But a cheese fondue is good for many other sorts of occasions and non-occasions, too. Après-ski—of course. Lunch in the big city—nice. In front of a roaring fire—beautiful. About midnight on Christmas Eve—it's becoming a tradition in our family. But don't rule out fondue just because it's summer or you live in a warm climate. It's not *that* warming.

I'm giving you a recipe that theoretically should serve four, or more if it's just for a snack. To me, it seems a more appropriate amount for two or three. If there are just one or two of you, you can cut the amounts in half if you don't feel too hungry.

1 clove garlic, cut in half	*A grind of black pepper*
1½ cups very dry white wine,	*A dash of nutmeg*
preferably Swiss Neuchatel	*3 tablespoons kirsch, combined*
1 tablespoon lemon juice	*with 1 tablespoon cornstarch*
1 pound grated or minced cheese	*A pinch of baking soda (optional)*
(see instructions below)	*Bread cubes*

Rub your fondue pot (or whatever you're using—an enameled cast-iron pot, for instance) with the garlic pieces. Discard the garlic. Heat the wine (Swiss Neuchatel is best, but any very dry white wine will do) in the pot on your regular kitchen stove to just below the boiling point. Add the lemon juice. Little by little, stir in the cheese. (An ideal combination is half Switzerland Swiss or Emmental and half natural Gruyère. But, again, use what you can get. All Switzerland Swiss or Emmental or even any hard, well-aged cheese of any sort.) When the cheese is melted (and don't worry if it hasn't quite combined with the wine), add the kirsch and cornstarch, which you've mixed together. Keep stirring—it'll all pull together. Now you're all set, but Spring Brothers suggest you add a pinch of baking soda (sodium bicarbonate). They say, "The Fondue will foam a little while but it becomes lighter and easier to digest." Worthy aims.

Now if you have a fondue burner, put the pot on it. Otherwise, eat fast! Serve with bread cubes—French or Italian bread cut in about 1-inch pieces, with some crust on each. See below for the procedure.

Some tips that Spring Brothers gave me:

If the fondue separates, a dash of vinegar will restore it.

Stir always in a figure-8 motion to prevent the cheese from getting stringy.

Urge all the eaters to stir the fondue with each piece they dunk. (If by chance you don't know how to eat fondue, I'll tell you in a minute.)

For newcomers to fondue: Put a bowlful of bread cubes on the table next to the fondue (a coffee table's nice for this). Each eater spears one cube of bread at a time with a fork (special fondue forks, if you have them). The bread is swished around in the fondue, then brought out with a swirling motion so that any strings of cheese that are dangling down end up on the bread. Or back in the pot. At any rate, not on the table and not on you. Then, because both fork and cheese are hot, push the cheese–bread cube off onto a plate. Eat it with another fork, a plain one this time.

There are some silly but fun traditions that go along with fondue. For instance, if your bread cube slips off your fork back into the pot, you're supposed to either provide a bottle of wine or kiss another diner of the opposite sex. More practical traditions involve serving white wine or kirsch, or tea, with your fondue.

Peach Jam and Cottage Cheese

A combination that means much to some people: a piece of toast (buttered or not, according to taste) with some peach jam and cottage cheese to put on it, bite by bite as it is eaten. It's one of those flavor and texture combinations that don't sound like much but really come off very well when tried. It makes a socially acceptable breakfast, but you might remember it for a comforting snack at other times of day, too.

Cottage Cheese with Wheat Germ

Cottage cheese with wheat germ is the contribution of our friend (unfortunately no relation) Avery Andrews. It's hardly a recipe: you just mix the honey-coated sort of wheat germ into some cottage cheese. Only a suggestion, but it does sound good, with the crunch of the wheat germ contrasting with the smoothness of the cheese.

Avery is a brilliant linguist, and this is his idea of the right food for times of mental or physical fatigue. He has also tried the crunchy sort of wheat germ mixed into yogurt, but says it was a disappointment and just didn't taste as good as he thought it would—too tangy. I suggested he add a little honey to it, but he reminded me that there's honey in that kind of wheat germ already. So I guess he's just going to stick to his cottage cheese and wheat germ. It should be a healthy diet, up to a point. (He eats other things, too. Ever since our daughter Katie first invited him to visit us years ago, he's been one of our favorite house guests. He's perfectly content to sleep on a sofa if we've run out of beds. You don't have to entertain him. But most important, he eats everything in sight, which is bound to endear him to a compulsive cook like me.)

VEGETABLES AND SALADS

GREENERY. Also reddery and a little yellowery. Many of these are mashes or mishmashes, because they're especially soothing and calming.

But certain moods benefit from vegetables cooked in other ways and from some salads. Thus, you'll find here such things as Pueblo Squash, which involves onions, cheese, tomatoes and sometimes peeled green chili as well as the squash. And crisp fried potatoes. And baked sliced onions and broiled sliced onions, both of which end up crunchy.

The salads all are on the sweet side. I *never* have a mood that is benefited by excess acidity—my moods are acid enough all by themselves. If you're different, I apologize.

Artichokes

I recently met a woman who has the interesting—especially gastronomically—background of having a French mother and a Middle-Eastern father. I asked her what food she most yearned for when she was tired or in need of solace, expecting some such answer as *"couscous"* or *"pâté de foie gras."* Instead, she replied, "Artichokes—hot, boiled artichokes with melted butter." And I could see it. This woman has a leisurely elegance, and I could visualize her slowly eating an artichoke, dipping each leaf in the butter, delicately removing the meat with her teeth, disposing of the choke with a deft stroke or two, cutting the heart into little pieces—and softly smiling all the while.

The more I thought about it, the more I could see myself doing it also, when the world became too much for me—only with not half her elegance.

First, trim off the very end of the artichokes' stems. Soak the artichokes for half an hour in salted water. Bring a big pot of water to a boil. Add about a tablespoon of salt, then your artichokes. Boil for about 45 minutes, depending on their size. They're done when a fork easily pierces the stem. Serve hot with melted butter or cold with mayonnaise.

Most people cut off all the stem so that the artichoke will stand up nicely on the plate. Since the stem is just about as tasty and tender as the heart, I'm willing to forgo looks for that extra goodness.

Barley as a Vegetable

Barley as a vegetable came into my life when I was making barley water (see page 212). When I came to the point toward the end of that process where you strain off the water, the cooked barley was left sitting in the strainer, looking very interesting. I threw it into a bowl, added butter, salt and pepper, and tasted it. Fabulous!

Cooked, buttered, salted and peppered barley tastes somewhat like wild rice, a bit like kasha, wheat pilaf and such. Cooked this way, it's still a little firm and chewy. You could quite profitably use it as a starchy vegetable with any sort of food, and it would be marvelous with shish kebab, especially topped with some of the basting sauce. In other words, use it as you would rice, and as you would use wild rice if you could afford it. I think I like it better than wild rice.

Make it just as in the recipe on page 212 and get a bonus of barley water, or cook it in about half as much water if you haven't been able to work up a taste for barley water. The total cooking time should be somewhere around a half hour. If you add enough butter, you'll be able to make it ahead and reheat it when needed.

The five little tablespoons of raw barley become a good-sized bowl of cooked barley, and I can just about guarantee you'll be crazy about it.

Purée of Green Beans

Delicious . . . smooth . . . beautiful to see . . . easy. What more could you ask of a vegetable?

1 package frozen green beans (any style) or ¾ pound fresh
1 very thin slice onion or 1 scallion, minced
2 tablespoons heavy cream
2 tablespoons milk
2 tablespoons butter
A dash of sugar
A good pinch of thyme
Salt, pepper and seasoned salt

Boil the green beans and the onion together in salted water until tender. If there's any water left, drain or boil it off. Put all the other ingredients in a blender container. Add the beans and onion. Blend until very smooth. Reheat, back in the pot, adding a little more butter and cream if you think they're needed, also more salt and pepper. Or if the purée's too thin, cook it down a bit. Also, if by any chance the beans were stringy, you're going to have to now put the purée through a sieve or food mill. This, to my intense dismay, turned out to be the case with some frozen beans recently. I'll never buy *that* brand again.

Serves 2 to 4.

Try these even though you don't usually like green beans. I know—in most cases when you're told things such as, "Even people who hate eggplant ask for second helpings when it's cooked this way," it turns out to just not be true. (Or at least I'm never able to get away with it with my children.) But this purée of green beans seems like a totally new vegetable. It's phenomenal.

Snibbled Beans

Sometimes I think snibbled beans are my favorite food. They're that good and that refreshing. I don't know what I'd do without them.

There seems to be a good bit of controversy as to what constitutes a properly snibbled bean. My version is derived from one that appeared in the *New York Times* several years ago, then in Jean Hewitt's *The New York Times Heritage Cook Book* (G. P. Putnam's Sons, 1972).

Green beans—1 pound fresh or   *3 slices bacon*
   one package frozen—Frenched,   *1 egg*
   cooked and drained; or 1 or 2   *¼ cup cider vinegar*
   cans, drained   *¼ cup sugar*
1 small onion, sliced paper-thin   *Salt and pepper to taste*

Put the drained beans into a frying pan or saucepan. Top with the sliced onion; set aside.

Cook the bacon until crisp. Drain on paper towels, then crumble onto the beans and onion. Pour off half the fat remaining in the bacon pan. To what's left (and it should be hot), add the egg, vinegar and sugar, which you've run together briefly in a blender or by hand.

Pour the mixture over the beans, etc. Toss like a salad. Now here's where the *Times* and I part company. I find that to achieve a sauce that seems thick enough to me, I have to cook and stir the whole thing for a minute or two more.

Add salt and pepper to taste, but because of the saltiness of the bacon, you may not need any extra.

Serves 2 to 4.

Marvelous as a meal, a main dish, a side dish or just a treat. A joy.

Frijoles Refritos

The Mexicans don't need any other sort of soothing food (though they do have some) as long as their cuisine includes *frijoles refritos* (refried beans). These smooth, bland beans temper the hotness of so many other Mexican foods. You'll often find them in tacos, tostadas and tamales and as side dishes with most other sorts of food—for breakfast, lunch, dinner or any time in between. *Frijoles refritos* cost so little, too, that they have a soothing effect on either the Mexican or Norte Americano food budget.

Good refried beans are available in cans, but to make them from scratch:

Wash and pick over ½ pound of pinto or pink beans, which are now becoming available all over the place, even in the Northeast. (Cut all these amounts in half or even in quarters if you want, but you might as well make a lot of these beans while you're at it; any you don't eat now will freeze nicely.) Or use any pink or red bean, even kidney beans. Put the beans in a pot with a lot of water. Throw away any that float on top. (They're hollow because nasty little wormlike creatures have been eating away at them.) Cover and simmer until the beans are tender—exceedingly tender—somewhere around 2 hours. Keep them covered with water until they're almost ready and keep the water simmering. If you're clever about this, and it's not hard, you'll end up with most of the liquid boiled off or absorbed at the same point the beans are done. Salt to taste.

These are the *frijoles,* cooked. Now to fry and refry them.

Put 3 to 4 tablespoons of lard, vegetable oil or bacon fat in a big skillet. When it's moderately hot, add the beans and their liquid, a spoonful at a time, mashing them with a fork as you go. Mash thoroughly or not, just as you prefer. Add more fat if they start to dry out too much. Now they're fried.

To refry, let them cool; then cook in additional fat until they're quite dry. I like them fairly creamy, but it's a creaminess that comes from the fat and the mashing.

Dress up the beans, if you wish, by adding, during the refrying, cubes of Monterey Jack cheese or strips of peeled green chili or bits of crisp bacon or bacon rind.

And don't tell, but a lot of people skip the second frying process and still call their beans *frijoles refritos.*

Baked Lima Beans

This was my grandmother's recipe, then my mother's, then mine and my children's. Maybe now it will be yours. It makes an excellent family tradition.

The lima beans in question are dried ones. They're cooked plain, then baked in a subtle, tangy sauce. They're good as a main dish, a vegetable or a snack—they're even good cold. (But then, that's true of any sort of baked beans.) And they're totally meat free. Why aren't more vegetarian dishes this satisfying and delicious?

½ cup dried lima beans

4 tablespoons butter, melted

½ cup sour cream

1 scant teaspoon dry mustard

½ tablespoon molasses

Soak and cook the lima beans: follow the directions on the package. (Or use 1 can of canned beans.) Combine with all the rest of the ingredients and bake in a buttered dish for 1½ hours at 350°, when the top will be brown and the sauce thick.

Maybe you'd better double this recipe, so you'll have some for breakfast, too. Or, with the double recipe, you could serve to 2 people as a main course or 4 to 6 as a vegetable.

Southern Connecticut Baked Beans

Well, they certainly aren't quite Boston Baked Beans by the time you get through doing all this to them. So from now on, they're going to be Southern Connecticut Baked Beans, because this is the way my mother used to do them all the years we lived there—in Greenwich, as far south in Connecticut as you can get. Mother never measured the ingredients, and neither do I—but I did just this once, so you'll know exactly where to start.

1 medium-size jar (18 ounces) or can Boston-style baked beans (see below)

2 tablespoons brown sugar

2 tablespoons minced onion

2 tablespoons cider vinegar

A pinch of dry mustard

2 strips bacon, cut in half

Combine all the ingredients except the bacon in an ovenproof dish—a smallish cast-iron skillet is perfect. If there are hunks of salt pork in the beans, chop them up a little. Lay the bacon strips on top. Bake at 325° until the bacon is brown and the beans are somewhat dry and crusted on top; about 1 hour. If you want to eat the beans sooner, cook them faster in a hotter oven. You can cook these beans fast or slow, cook them earlier and reheat them or do just about whatever you want with them.

Serves 2 to 4.

The beans I use are B&M Brick Oven Baked Beans. Use whatever kind you like, but I'd stay away from the tomato-sauce type beans for this. The cider vinegar is important. "Essential," I would have said, except for the fact that the last time I made these beans my cider vinegar had disappeared (into a scientific experiment of my youngest child, no doubt); so I used malt vinegar, and it was almost as good. Almost, but not quite! But malt vinegar's hard to find except in southern Delaware, where they serve it on French fried potatoes, and in Canada. Tarragon or wine vinegar would be all wrong.

If you taste these beans before they're cooked, you may think there's too much vinegar. Don't worry: it evaporates as it cooks. I use a little more than this, actually, but I didn't want to scare you off.

Sweet and Sour Cabbage

Not all cabbage tastes like what Maggie and Jiggs have done all that battling about.

Here's a version that tastes more like Chinese Sweet and Pungent Pork. It doesn't smell up your house, either. Try it when you're sick and tired of all the things you usually eat; it will perk up your jaded taste buds.

2 cups shredded cabbage, regular
  or Chinese celery cabbage
1 small onion, coarsely chopped
½ small green pepper, coarsely
  chopped
2 tablespoons vegetable oil

½ teaspoon salt
½ plus ⅓ cup water
1 teaspoon cornstarch
1 tablespoon cider vinegar
1 tablespoon sugar

Cook the cabbage, onion and green pepper in the oil for 2 or 3 minutes. Add the salt and the ½ cup of water and simmer, stirring, for another 2 or 3 minutes. Combine the cornstarch, vinegar, sugar and the ⅓ cup water. Add to the pan and simmer and stir for another few minutes, until the sauce has thickened and become transparent.

Serves 3 or 4.

Adding a little green pepper whenever you cook cabbage or other odoriferous vegetables is a fine trick to know about. It adds to the flavor, of course, but best of all, it eliminates the usual pungent smell. You can be a secret cabbage-eater anytime at all, and no one will know.

Mashed Carrots

There seem to be a number of people who consider mashed carrots the top soothing food of them all. How, I used to think, could they possibly find them soothing when just mashing the carrots would make a wreck out of anyone? The secret, I have now figured out, is overcooking the carrots. None of this crisp-tender stuff that's so good with carrots cooked other ways. Falling apart is the stage you want for this purpose; then they'll mash nicely.

2 *cups peeled and thinly sliced carrots*

Salted water to cover very amply

2 *to 4 tablespoons butter*

2 *to 4 tablespoons heavy cream*

2 *to 4 tablespoons milk*

A speck of sugar (that's smaller than a dash)

A trace of nutmeg or ginger (that's smaller than a speck)

Salt and pepper

Boil the carrots in the water until the water is all gone and the carrots are very, very soft. If the water disappears before the carrots are soft enough, just pour in some more and carry on.

Now mash—with the kind of potato masher that has holes in the bottom or the kind that doesn't (usually made of wood) or with a food mill. Even with a spoon or fork. Add butter and cream and milk as you go, using the larger amounts, or even more, if you want a melt-in-your-mouth mash. Add the seasonings, using more sugar and spice if you like. Reheat if necessary, stirring carefully. Eat.

This, I guess, is where I should make the apology I feel I owe to the food mill manufacturers. I bought myself first an American-made food mill, then a French one, and I couldn't seem to make either one of the blasted things work. They seemed to involve terrible drudgery and little in the way of results. Unfortunately, I made a snide remark or two to this effect in another book. Well, food mill people, I was an idiot. All these years I have been putting the discs into my food mills upside down, which isn't easy to do, I might add. They never had a chance to function properly. So let me now say loudly and clearly that food mills, once you get over being a klutz and put them together right, work just beautifully.

Caribbean Carrots

These are sweet carrots, but with crazy undertones of citrus and spice and everything nice—including rum. They are mouth-watering.

2 cups carrots, peeled and thinly sliced
¾ cup water
¾ cup orange juice
¼ cup sugar
Coarsely grated rind of ½ lemon
2 whole cloves

A dash of nutmeg
Salt (no pepper, for once)
2 teaspoons rum (I like a dark rum for this, but any kind will do)
1 tablespoon chopped chives (optional)

Put everything except the rum and chives into a pot. Boil rather quickly until the carrots are done and the liquid has become a thick syrup. Fish out and throw away the whole cloves. Add the rum, then cook for a few minutes more. This gets rid of the alcoholic content; if you don't find that desirable, skip this step. Stir in the chives, if you're using them (some people like them with this, some don't, so try a few on a spoonful of carrots and syrup before you make an irreversible decision).

Serves 2 to 4.

There's another version of these carrots in which you do all this, let the carrots sit all night in their syrup, drain them and then fry them in butter. Since Caribbean carrots are so good just boiled as above, I haven't felt the need to try this more complicated version, but you might want to.

Note to my friend Barbara Ingraham: This is, of course, the

recipe you've been asking me for for several years now, and I never got around to writing out before!

Purée of Chestnuts

Or *purée de marrons,* to be very French about this—and it's canned French *marrons* I suggest you use for this recherché, utterly luxurious treat. Coping with chestnuts in the shell is too exhausting for people who need soothing already—unless you're indulging in a feast of roasted chestnuts (page 227).

> Drain the liquid from canned chestnuts. Mash them with a fork or masher or put through a food mill. Heat gently, stirring, with a couple of tablespoons each of butter and heavy cream, until the purée is hot and fluffy. Season with salt and black pepper.

You can eat this by itself—and by yourself—as a feast for one. Or serve it as a side dish with such festive foods as, for instance, goose. When I used to have my hair done at Elizabeth Arden in New York, *purée de marrons* was the favorite status-indicating subject of conversation of the gabbling clientele all through the holiday season. It's good in spite of that.

Camper's Corn

So-called because it's a great dish to cook when you're camping out. But good for indoor types and indoor moments, too, and a fine thing for a quick meal when everything else you can think of seems too demanding.

3 slices bacon, diced   2 eggs
2 tablespoons diced onion   Salt and pepper
1 buffet-size can cream-style corn

> Cook the bacon and onion together in a medium-sized skillet until both are brown. Pour off all but about 1 tablespoon of bacon fat. If your bacon's lean enough, there won't be more fat than that, and if that's the case, drop me a line about where you buy your bacon, will you? Add the corn and stir until it's heated. Now add the eggs, unbeaten, and stir until they're set and the mixture has thickened. Season with salt and pepper.

There may be times you'd like this better without the onion. Why not? And other times you'd like to add something else; chopped, peeled green chilies would be wonderful in this, and so would grated cheese. So would lots of things—but nothing more is actually needed.

Braised Endive

Braised endive has quite a sophisticated taste. Almost acrid; not quite bitter. Save it for an ascetic mood, when anything bland or rich would be offensive. It's one of my favorite foods, but only for times when I'm surfeited with the good life and its overrich food.

> For each serving, put 3 endives side by side in a well-buttered pan. (If you cook these in quantity, keep them in just 1 layer.) Dot with 1 tablespoon of butter, sprinkle on the juice of ½ lemon and add about 3 tablespoons of chicken broth or water. Cover with but-

tered wax paper, then a lid. Bake at 325° for about 45 minutes.

The endive in question is the Belgian sort, white and spindle-shaped, not the green, spike-edged chicory that sometimes bears the noble name of endive.

Leeks and Endive Stewed in Butter

Leeks as a vegetable are beautiful. (Boil them sometime and serve them like asparagus with melted butter or hollandaise.) Endive, too. (See the previous recipe.) Together, stewed in butter, they're extremely rewarding, particularly when your mood calls for a vegetable, but not a bland, puréed one—and when you don't want to wait: this is a quick dish.

Shave off the root end of 1 or 2 leeks, and remove all the green part. Wash what remains thoroughly, then cut into ½-inch lengths. Now the endives: shave off the root end of 1 or 2 of these, too, then cut what's left into pieces about the same size as the leek segments. Stir for a couple of minutes in a frying pan with 2 or 3 tablespoons of butter; cover and simmer for 10 minutes or so. Add about 1 teaspoon of lemon juice and a sprinkling of salt.
Serves 1 to 3.

For a change, and a pretty one, substitute cubes of red or green pepper for the leeks, or for the endive. Or combine these any old way, or cook any of them alone by this method. You'll be entranced.

Lettuce with Sugar

It was fun for me to read recently another author's opinion that one of the nice things about eating alone is that you can have sugar on your lettuce. I know just what he means. Sugared lettuce is a culinary sacrilege that you really shouldn't let anyone know you indulge in. But hush, hush! . . . It's delicious.

> The recipe? Don't be silly. Put the cut-up (torn apart, really) lettuce in a bowl. Sprinkle with sugar. How much? Oh, 1 or 2 tablespoons should take care of enough lettuce to serve one person. Don't add anything else at all.

Putting sugar on your lettuce is a simple way to be a happy sinner—and with far less repercussions than most.

Lettuce with Sour Cream and Sugar

I suppose true gourmets would cringe at this form of salad just about as much as at the plainer lettuce with sugar of the previous recipe. But the sour cream provides just enough tartness and smoothness to make a nice, easy-on-the-nerves salad.

> For 2 cups of torn-apart lettuce, combine ¼ cup of sour cream and 2 teaspoons of sugar. Mix well with the lettuce and chill for a while, if you have the time. Start out with more lettuce than you think, as it compresses and seems to shrink when it's bearing this heavy a dressing.

Yogurt should be good in this, too, instead of sour cream. I just haven't tried it yet. I wonder how some of the fruit-flavored yogurts would work out with lettuce? At the very least, they should be interesting. I do know, though, that adding perhaps 2 teaspoons of lemon juice and the grated rind of half a lemon to the sour cream is just as delicious—and quite different.

Wilted Lettuce

Wilted lettuce is very good for wilted people, and for those with the feeling that they absolutely can't face one more green salad. It's neither hot nor cold, neither sweet nor sour, neither totally limp nor totally crisp. As Goldilocks would have said, it's *just right*.

> Cook 3 slices of bacon until crisp. Drain on paper towels, then crumble. To the fat remaining in the pan, add 1 tablespoon of cider vinegar, ½ tablespoon of granulated sugar and 2 tablespoons of chopped scallion or minced onion. Cook together briefly; then add the crumbled bacon and pour—while still very hot— over enough torn-apart leaf lettuce (romaine, Boston, bibb or some such) to serve one as a whole meal or two or more as a side dish. Use more lettuce than you think you need: it shrinks as it "wilts."

Some brave souls—true vinegar-lovers—omit the sugar entirely. Some use brown sugar. A few add cream, sweet or sour, or even garlic, of all things. A large number add a little water; I guess I do, too, if you count the water that's usually clinging to my lettuce leaves.

Wilted spinach is good. Just switch the greens and keep everything else the same.

Braised Lettuce in Cream

A surprise to most Americans, the very existence of such a dish as braised lettuce. It's a French idea that hasn't been very widely circulated here.

It's always sounded appealing to me, but I only tried it recently on one evening when I was tired and somewhat frazzled and suddenly realized that braised lettuce was the one thing I wanted to eat. Ridiculous . . . How could I crave something I'd never tasted? But I did. (If I'm like this at this stage of my life, can you imagine what my cravings were like the three times I was pregnant? Actually, I had very few then, or at least I didn't indulge them then as much as I do now.)

French cookbooks abound in braised lettuce recipes, but all the ones I found seemed too complicated, so here's what I did.

Cut up about 3 or 4 times as much lettuce as you would use for a salad for one person. Put it in a saucepan with 1 tablespoon or a little more of butter. Cook and stir for 2 or 3 minutes. Add about 4 tablespoons of cream. Simmer, stirring now and then, until the cream has been almost absorbed. Season with salt and pepper

To serve more, simply multiply everything.

Simple . . . smooth . . . rich . . . good. Everything I hoped and thought it would be. Trust your cravings.

Baked Sliced Onions

According to the folklore of a number of countries, onions are medicinal, whether they're used internally or externally. There were stories during World War II that the Russians were slicing up onions and putting them on open wounds. Much scoffing from our medics, until they saw how beautifully the wounds were healing. My father has told me that Swedish people in Minnesota used to pick up raw onions in the fields and eat them as the rest of us might bite on an apple, and that this gave them great strength. And then there are cold cures based on the onion. This is not a medical book, and I'm certainly not suggesting you try any of these onion remedies as such, but it does seem to me that a plateful of cooked onions just somehow does make me feel better when I'm coming down with something (as long as the something doesn't involve my stomach). This is one of the ways I like them best.

> Slice the onions fairly thin. Put them into a buttered casserole in layers, sprinkling each layer with a little brown sugar and some dabs of butter. Bake at 350°, uncovered, for about 1 hour.

Use lots of onions (two big ones per person is about right), since they shrink considerably as they cook and since they're tremendously good.

Broiled Onion Slices with Sour Cream

When an onion-craving mood overcomes you, try these simple, sweet slices.

Cut Bermuda onions into ½-inch slices. Cook them gently in butter for 10 minutes or so, covered. Turn them once or twice. They shouldn't brown at all. Then put them in a broiling pan and on top of each put a tablespoon of sour cream into which you've mixed a hefty pinch of dried dill weed or chopped fresh dill. Spread the cream out until it covers most of each slice. Sprinkle on a little paprika. Broil for just a few minutes, or until the slices look as delicious as they're going to taste.

When you're not making a full meal out of these onion slices, try them with steaks, chops or any simply-cooked meat. They'll dazzle you.

The Crispest Fried Potatoes

If you like the outside of French-fried potatoes—the crisp part—the best, then these are the potatoes for you. There's very little inside compared to crust in each piece. They're certainly the ones for me.

I've found them soothing on more than one occasion. My first year in college I met a delightful girl named Mary Griffith. "Griff" was the perfect person to do double-crostics and other such nonsense with. Somehow, though, in our fooling around, we hurt the feelings of a rather prissy girl named Beverly. So to show us, Beverly gave a party in her room and invited everyone on that floor of the dorm except us. This struck us funny— you see the sort of ridiculous people we were then—so we had a party of our own, just the two of us. There was a little kitchenette just opposite Beverly's room, and in it we cooked a tremendous panful of these potatoes, lacing them with onion just to make sure the smell would be pervading. Most of the party ended up with us—to our delight—which just shows what horrid girls we truly were.

> Even if you're making these marvelous potatoes just for yourself, use one quite large potato or two small ones. Nowadays I don't peel the potato; in my college days I did. It really doesn't matter. Cube the potatoes into small pieces, maybe ⅜-inch square. At college this used to take me half an hour. Now I slice the potatoes, stack them and cut down through them, first one way, then the other, which takes practically no time at all. Heat fat in a frying pan big enough to cook the potatoes in one layer. You can use any fat (I used to use white vegetable shortening, but now it's more apt to be vegetable oil) and use enough to come up about halfway on the potatoes. Fry, stirring from time to time, until the cubes are brown and gorgeous. Drain on paper towels, sprinkle with salt and try to get them onto a plate before you eat them all up.

About the chopped onion Griff and I added. It's a good addition, but you have to remember to put it in after the potatoes have cooked for a bit. Otherwise the onion will burn before the potatoes have gotten brown, and that's not nice at all.

Mashed Potatoes

"I'm rather a mashed potato person," a friend told me when I asked her what foods she found the most soothing. Well, there are a lot of mashed potato people around. I'm one, myself. Call these potatoes "whipped" or "creamed," or anything else that occurs to you. They're basic, smooth, infinitely satisfying.

The real thing, the honest-to-goodness, homemade mashed potato, is hard to handle when you have dinner guests, since it really should be made at the last minute, unless it's to be part of another dish. But when you are cooking to soothe, you and anyone else you are coping with will, no doubt, be ready to eat whenever the potatoes are done—unless, perhaps, you're in the middle of a soothing martini.

1 pound potatoes (strangely enough, "baking" potatoes are best for this)
4 to 5 tablespoons (or more) butter, softened

⅓ cup heavy cream, heated
Salt and pepper (white pepper disappears but flavors)

Peel the potatoes, cut them into pieces about 1 x 2 inches and boil them in lightly salted water to well cover until they are soft. This won't take long. Test by poking them with the end of a sharp knife: when they no longer fight back, they're done. Drain, then return to the cooking pot and stir or shake over lowish heat until they're thoroughly dry. (This step is very important, dumb as it may sound.)

Now mash. How? In a ricer, maybe, or with a masher, though you may have to put the potatoes through a food mill or strainer after this step. The best bet is a good mixer. Twirl the potatoes in this until they're very smooth before adding anything. Whatever, don't use a blender for this particular operation.

All mashed? OK. Now add the butter, a tablespoon at a time. Then the heated heavy cream, also just 1 tablespoon at a time. Then the salt and pepper. And serve *pronto*.

If you don't have heavy cream, you can still make lovely mashed potatoes. The best way is to use milk and some sour cream. If you're out of sour cream, too, you're in bad shape, but you can make do by using less milk than you would cream and adding at least a tablespoon or two more butter.

Boiled New Potatoes

I don't know what they fed my daughter Katie at college, but she used to come home craving boiled new potatoes, especially the red ones. It got so I'd have to make sure to have some on hand as her vacation times drew near. They seemed to mean "home and Mother" to her, and I'm not sure I enjoy being thought of as a potato. Oh, well—I guess it beats being symbolized by apple pie, the legendary fate of the American "Mom."

I won't insult you by telling you how to boil a potato. If you can boil water, you've got it made. Just salt the water, use the smallest possible potatoes and poke a fork into one of the largest of the potatoes to see if they're done.

Serve unpeeled with an ample supply of butter, salt and pepper. Or get fancy (but why?) and pull off a strip of peel around each potato's middle; then roll the little tubers in melted butter mixed with chopped parsley and perhaps chives or other fresh herbs.

Hashed in Cream Potatoes

Many good restaurants, particularly in California, make a big thing of Hashed in Cream Potatoes, but it's hard to find a recipe for them—which is a shame, since everyone should know how good they are. They shouldn't be reserved for the very rich and the Hollywood types; all the rest of us need this sort of soothing, too.

2 *medium-size potatoes*	*½ cup cream*
2 *tablespoons butter*	*A dash of nutmeg*
½ teaspoon flour	*Salt and pepper*

Bake the potatoes until they're almost but not quite done—until, in other words, they're still somewhat firm. Cool the potatoes, peel them and chop them into small dice.

Make a cream sauce: Melt one tablespoon of the butter. Remove from the fire and stir in the flour, then the cream. Cook and stir until the sauce bubbles. Mix the cubed potatoes into this. Season with the nutmeg, salt and pepper to taste.

Put into a buttered baking dish. Dot the top of the potato mixture with the remaining tablespoon of butter. Bake at 350° until the top is a pretty speckled brown.

Marvelous as a meal all by itself or with a simply cooked meat. Steak, for instance, or great restaurant-size slabs of rare roast beef.

Fried Potato Skins

Some wonderful people named Moore used to live near us in Connecticut. They often gave summer-Sunday noontime picnics at a small lake back in their woods. I can still see Aunt Betty

Moore doing such a careful, sedate breast stroke across the lake that not a single drop of water splashed onto her elaborately coiffed hair or even on her diamond earrings. Uncle Arthur, her husband, smiled fondly and said, "Here comes Betty, swimming to the opera."

And I can still see Uncle Arthur, who looked a good bit like Teddy Roosevelt, standing at the fire before a big iron skillet, stirring potato skins for us to eat while we sat around on rocks, looked at the lake and waited for the steak and fried potatoes that were to come. Such happy days.

So these are my memories and the mood evoked when I eat fried potato skins these days. Try them yourself and make your own memories.

> Use thin skins if possible, ones you've shaved from washed potatoes with a vegetable peeler. They can be large pieces or small; it doesn't matter. Heat about ¼ inch of bacon or sausage fat in a frying pan. Add the pieces of potato skin and stir until they are brown and crisp. Drain on paper towels. Sprinkle with salt.

If you don't want to eat the potatoes from which you've obtained the skins the same day, store them in water in your refrigerator (though this is said to destroy some of the nutrients) or boil them now and chill, then chop and fry them the next day.

Baked Potatoes

There come moments in the life of almost everyone when the only possible food is a baked potato. These are mainly moments of mental fatigue following too much work at a desk (writing, for instance) or too much worry. A baked potato will help you relax, and the cooking of it won't wear you out in the least. Here's my idea of the perfect baked potato.

Scrub a medium-size Idaho or California potato. Cut a sliver off one end. Rub the potato with soft butter. Bake at 375° or 400° until the skin of the potato is darkened and its contours have changed, until it has developed dimples, more or less. If you grab the potato with a pot holder and squeeze it, it will give. Allow at least 45 minutes for it to reach this point.

If you're serving someone else aside from yourself, cut a small cross in the top of the potato. Then, using a pot holder, push in and up on each of the potato's 4 corners. This will make the top pop open within the cross you've cut. Slip a pat of butter into this opening. Serve with extra butter, salt and pepper.

But if you're your only potato customer, just cut the potato in half, put on lots of butter and salt and pepper, grab a fork and start mashing the meat of the potato. Eat the skin too—it's the best part.

For fancy baked potatoes, top them, after they're cooked and cut open, with sour cream mixed with minced scallions, chives or onions . . . or Welsh Rabbit (see page 94) . . . or crisp, crumbled bacon . . . or Creamed Chipped Beef (see page 40) . . . or grated cheese . . . or make them into Stuffed Baked Potatoes, the following recipe.

Stuffed Baked Potatoes

This is the make-ahead version of the baked potato. It's also a good bit fancier and more of a potato-to-be-served-to-guests.

So these potatoes are for the days when you know ahead of time that you'll be limp by evening or when you have other brain-weary souls to comfort with food.

Bake the potatoes as detailed in the previous recipe. Cut them in two—I do it lengthwise, but some prefer to make the cut across the middle. If each half doesn't sit nicely and evenly, cut a small piece off the bottom. Then scoop out most of the insides, leaving just a shell of skin and pulp. Mash the pulp with butter and hot milk (see page 120) and add goodies. Any or several of these: chopped scallions, onions or chives; crumbled bacon; herbs (just a pinch or two of marjoram or sage, for instance); minced sautéed garlic; grated cheese; or anything else that strikes your fancy.

Stuff the potato shells with this mixture. Swirl the top with a fork. Sprinkle on a little paprika or grated cheese. The potatoes can now sit until you're ready to eat them. Just reheat at 400° for about 10 minutes when you want them.

This is also a good way to save a calorie or two and make one potato serve two people, or the same person twice. You can eat one half now and freeze the other for another brain-tiring day.

Baked Sweet Potatoes

It's one of life's more unfathomable mysteries to me why more people don't cook—or even seem to have heard of—baked sweet potatoes. Just plain old baked-in-the-skin sweet potatoes, well drenched in butter and liberally salted and peppered. With pork chops, with broiled chicken, with anything at all or without anything else. They're a perfect food when you want something that's hot and smooth and has a natural sweetness, and when you don't want to expend much strength on fixing it.

> Scrub the potatoes. Dry them and butter the skins well. (Don't, don't, don't skip this step. A sweet potato that explodes all over your oven because the skin was too stiff to give with the expanding inside part is a dreadful experience. If you don't want to use butter, though, you can cut a slice off one end of the potato instead.) Bake at 350° or so until done. Sorry I can't tell you how long; it depends on the size of the sweet potato. "Done" is when you grab a sweet potato with a pot holder, give it a squeeze (gently!) and it feels soft.

Now sit yourself down, preferably in front of a going fireplace. Have lots of butter handy and some salt and a pepper mill. Open your potato up and start adding butter and mashing with a fork. Mash the salt and pepper in, too. Now eat this ambrosia, skin and all, watch the flames in the fireplace shoot up and down and change color—and you'll be wonderfully limp and relaxed. Try to at least put the rest of the butter away before you go to sleep.

Baked Rutabagas

I'm really not much of a fan of rutabagas, those huge yellow turnips eaten by cattle in Europe and human beings in the United States. Or at least I wasn't until I tried baking them in their skins; then they became a whole new vegetable, totally unlike the bitter, horrid, boiled or mashed yellow turnip of hate-

ful memory. Try them this way when you have a strong urge
to feel of-the-earth-earthy.

> Scrub your rutabaga—the smallest one you can find—
> very thoroughly in the hottest water you can stand.
> This will remove the preservative wax coating. Cut
> a sliver off each end. Rub the skin with butter or oil.
> Bake the rutabaga at 400°, or any other convenient
> temperature, until a fork poked in meets no resistance.
> Cut the turnip in half, then serve just as you would
> a baked potato, with butter, salt and pepper.

There's no real reason why you couldn't add the sour cream
and so forth that can go on a fancy baked potato, but if you do,
you make them rather elegant, and can you imagine an elegant
rutabaga?

Creamed, Buttered Spinach

When my daughter Katie was very small, I tried to explain
Lent to her. Part of what I said was that people often gave up
their very favorite food for Lent—candy, for instance, or ice
cream, or whatever it was. Katie thought a minute and then said,
"Well, spinach is what I like better than anything in the world,
so I guess that's what I'd better give up." And so it was. For the
entire Lenten period, Katie ate no spinach—and neither did
any of the rest of us since, of course, I didn't have the heart to
even have it in the house. After Lent we went on a spinach binge.

> Use 1 pound of fresh spinach or a package of frozen,
> chopped spinach. If fresh, wash it, discard the tough
> stems, blanch it for 4 or 5 minutes in boiling salted

water to more than amply cover, drain and chop. If frozen, put it in a pan and let it almost completely thaw; then boil off its juices.

By either method, you now have cooked, chopped spinach. Reheat it with 1 tablespoon of butter, then remove from the heat and slowly stir in ⅓ cup of heavy cream. Heat gently, stirring often, until the cream has been absorbed. Remove from the heat; stir in another tablespoon of butter; season with salt and pepper and perhaps a bit of spice. Everybody uses nutmeg—why don't you be the first person on your block to use cinnamon in your spinach? Or an herb— rosemary for instance. Or nothing—that's what I've been adding to my spinach lately. Quite unusual, and very nice.

Serves 2 or 3.

Jane Grigson, in her charming book *Good Things,* tells of "Four Day Spinach," in which the delectable greens are cooked, chopped, lavishly buttered and chilled. For the next two days you heat the spinach up, add a lot more butter and then chill it again. On the fourth day you heat and butter, but this time you get to eat the spinach. It sounds fascinating, but I don't think I could ever resist eating the spinach for three whole days. So I stick to cooking it this way, or I season with butter and cider vinegar, an old Middle Western, or possibly German, trick.

Spinach Soufflé

I've told you how my daughter Katie loves spinach so much she once gave it up for Lent. Well, my son, Bob, also likes it, though he doesn't go to such extremes about it. His idea of how to eat spinach is in a soufflé, and I think he'd be happy to have it every night of his life. (Candy, my other daughter, has more of the "I say it's spinach, and I say I hate it" approach to the subject.)

You can make a spinach soufflé by following any basic non-sweet soufflé recipe, adding about 1 cup of well-drained spinach and 1 or 2 tablespoons of minced onion. But for an easier, quicker and still good way:

4 tablespoons butter
4 tablespoons flour
1 cup milk
1 cup cooked and chopped spinach (or use 1 package of frozen chopped spinach, thawed and well drained)

1 egg, unbeaten
Salt and pepper
A dash of nutmeg
½ cup grated cheese (optional)
1 tablespoon minced onion (optional)

Make a white sauce by melting the butter, stirring in the flour, and mixing in the milk very thoroughly. Cook and stir over low heat until the sauce is quite thick. Cool slightly. Add the spinach, the egg and the seasonings. Bake at 350° for 45 minutes.

Serves 3 or 4.

An optional addition: a half-cup of grated cheese (Cheddar, Swiss or Parmesan) stirred into the white sauce just before you add the spinach and egg. Another: a tablespoon of minced onion, added at the same time.

Note that where this recipe differs from the usual soufflé is that you use only one egg, and it doesn't have to be separated and beaten. This makes a lot of difference to the cook, but changes the soufflé very little.

Bob really cherishes his spinach soufflé and didn't take kindly to the idea of my putting cheese into it, but he had to admit that it's pretty good this way, too.

Purée of Winter Squash

Mashed winter squash speaks of pilgrim days in New England and pioneer days in the West. It can see you through a hard winter, or just a difficult day.

1 small winter squash (see recipe)	*Sugar*
Butter	*Salt and pepper*
Ginger	*Heavy cream*

You can use any winter squash—butternut, Hubbard, golden nugget—or whatever you can find, even pumpkin. If it's unavoidably a big squash, just use part of it. Peel the squash and cut it into small pieces, perhaps only ½-inch cubes. Place in a saucepan and barely cover with water. Cover and boil till the squash is very tender. This will take a remarkably short time because of the smallness of the pieces. At this point, if there's still water in the pot, boil it off.

Now add 1 tablespoon of butter and start mashing with a fork as you stir the butter in. This is the easiest mashing you've ever had anything to do with. Add a little more butter. Mash some more. Add a dash of ginger, 1 teaspoon of sugar and a little salt and pepper. Taste. Not quite right? All right, keep going. Add more butter, more sugar, even a little more ginger, salt and pepper. When it tastes marvelous enough, add a tablespoon or two of heavy cream.

Serves 1 or 2.

If this doesn't seem meal enough to you all by itself, serve some pan-fried sausages with it. The flavors and textures are wonderfully complementary.

Pueblo Squash

Here is summer squash as prepared by many New Mexicans, only they're more apt to call it *calabacitas,* and what they use is usually zucchini. In coolish weather, towns like Santa Fe smell marvelous. It's a combination, I think, of piñon wood burning in adobe fireplaces and the cooking of blue tortillas and such dishes as this. These squash dishes seem, like practically everything else in New Mexico, to be a heritage from both the Indians and the Spanish, in equal parts.

1 medium summer squash or zucchini, diced, unpeeled
1 small onion, chopped
1 tablespoon butter
1 small can tomatoes, drained, or 1 fresh tomato, peeled, seeded and chopped

1 canned peeled green chili, minced, or a dash or two of hot pepper sauce (optional)
¼ pound Monterey Jack cheese, minced or shredded (no Monterey Jack?—use a natural Cheddar)
Salt and, perhaps, pepper

Sauté the squash and onions in the butter until both begin to soften. Add the tomatoes and, if you like, the green chili or hot pepper sauce. Simmer together until everything is tender; then stir in the cheese and cook for 2 or 3 minutes more. The cheese should be somewhat stringy, stretching its tentacles over everything. Add salt to taste and, if you think it needs it, a speck or two of pepper.

If you're serving this as a side dish for two instead of a whole dinner for one, you can use half this amount of cheese; then it won't overpower the rest of the meal. Serves 1 or 2.

Pueblo squash will always bring back New Mexico to me, and I was very happy there both as a child and on a recent trip. You don't need these connotations, though, to enjoy it. All you need is the wish to have something quiet, soft, mildly piquant and delicious. It's also one of the vegetarian dishes most likely to satisfy meat-eaters.

The Coolest Tomatoes

Anything combined with sugar before chilling seems to become amazingly cold. These tomatoes are the most cooling ever, and perfect for any time when ice cold tomatoes might appeal if it weren't for their usual acidity. They're perfect for the worst day a hot summer can inflict on you.

Peel and seed the ripest tomatoes you can find; cut them into chunks or wedges. Sprinkle with 1 teaspoon each of sugar and tarragon vinegar and a pinch of dried tarragon or ¼ teaspoon of the fresh for each tomato. Stir gently. Chill for at least 1 hour.

It may be hard to believe, but these tomatoes were inspired by a Chinese recipe. The tarragon, though, is a Western touch.

Creamed Tomatoes

My mother and I discovered these at a time when we were under a great strain, testifying, through no fault of our own, in a law suit. We were staying in someone else's house. Scrounging through the cookbooks there after the first day in court, not really feeling like eating anything, we came across this recipe— and found all the ingredients in the refrigerator. We liked the creamed tomatoes so much and found them so right for the occasion that we ate them as our entire dinner for the next three nights. I've learned since that they are also known as Pennsylvania Dutch tomatoes—to the surprise, I suspect, of the Pennsylvania Dutch.

2 tomatoes, fairly ripe	*3 tablespoons brown sugar*
Flour for dredging	*4 tablespoons heavy cream*
4 tablespoons butter	*Salt and pepper*

Cut the tomatoes into slices about ½ inch thick. (Don't peel the tomatoes first; just remove the stem end.) Dip both sides of the slices into flour, then fry in the butter, which should be sizzling. When the first side has browned, sprinkle the top with half of the brown sugar; then turn the slices over and turn the heat down to low. Sprinkle on the other half of the brown sugar. You may have to add more butter and turn the slices several times to achieve the proper brownness without burning the brown sugar. When the tomato slices are brown on both sides and the butter and brown sugar have become a lovely caramelized mess, stir in the cream. Season to taste with salt and pepper. Either serve at once or keep hot on a warming tray. The slices will lose their shape, but that doesn't matter in the least.

Serves 1 or 2.

Actually, you can make quite a successful version of this dish with canned tomatoes. Cook the butter and brown sugar together until they are slightly caramelized, then add the other ingredients and cook for about 5 minutes. Allow 1 small can of tomatoes and 2 tablespoons of flour for the regular amounts of the other things.

Fried Green Tomatoes

Fried green tomatoes are about as down-home a dish as you could find. I suppose it's for that reason that those of us with a bit of the Midwest in our background tend to turn to them. Maybe it's just because fried green tomatoes (especially with cream gravy—fried green tomatoes are unthinkable without it) taste so good and so different from other foods. When you want these tomatoes, nothing else is going to satisfy you. This could lead to great frustration if you don't have access to green tomatoes, but in that case, you can get by with the half-ripe tomatoes that are what you find in most markets anyway.

2 green tomatoes	*2 tablespoons flour*
Flour for dredging	*About 1 cup milk*
3 to 4 tablespoons butter, oil, lard or bacon fat	*Salt and freshly ground black pepper*

Slice the tomatoes about ⅓ inch thick. Dip them into a plateful of flour. Heat the fat in a skillet. This can be any sort of fat—butter, oil, lard or bacon fat—but if you use bacon fat and make it right before you cook the tomatoes, you'll have bacon to serve with your fried green tomatoes, and that's a nice combination. The bacon fat adds good flavor, too, though you might want to add a little vegetable oil to it so it won't burn and so the dish won't add too much saturated fat to your life.

Fry the tomatoes over fairly low heat, turning them now and then, until they are brown on both sides and soft in the middle. Remove them to a warm plate while you quickly make the cream gravy.

Pour off all but about 2 tablespoons of fat. Add an equal amount of flour. Cook and stir this for a minute or two, then start adding the milk. (Yes, you use milk, but rich milk, not skim, to make cream gravy.) Keep on cooking, stirring and adding milk until the cream gravy is—how can I describe it?—a little less thick than mayonnaise. This will take about 1 cup of milk, maybe more. Season well with salt and pepper. Pour onto the tomatoes.

If you serve this with any other food, make it something very simple and unsauced: plain baked or fried ham, grilled sausage or something like that.

Baked Tomatoes

This is a secret recipe. At any rate, it *was* a secret. My mother gave it to me. She learned about it from a friend whose father told her about it, and he was the one who broke the faith and broke the secret wide open. The father, so I was told, belonged to a club of male epicures in Philadelphia. This group put together a small book of the members' best recipes. Each member received a copy, but was supposed to never, ever give the recipes to anyone else. So much for *that* secret. Anyway, it's much too good a recipe to be kept hidden away. However, knowing what happens when any piece of information passes from person to person, it's very possible that the originator wouldn't recognize it at all now.

Use 1 whole, unskinned tomato for each person. Cut out the stem and place each tomato in an individual baking dish. Cut down deeply through the stem ends, making 2 cuts that form a cross or an ×. Open the tomato up so it forms a four-petaled flower (more or less).

Top with chopped onion, brown sugar and butter. The amounts you use don't seem to be too important, and I've never measured them. (That's one of the nice things about word-of-mouth recipes.) I'd say, at a rough guess, that for each tomato I use about ½ a medium-size onion, chopped or minced. On that I put about 2 tablespoons of brown sugar (I use dark brown) and on that, about 1 tablespoon of butter.

Then into the oven, at 350° or so, for at least a half hour. ("The longer the better," Mother said, and come to think of it, I guess she also said they should bake at a low temperature. I've cooked them at 300° and at 450° and at about every temperature in-between, and they've been delicious every time.)

One of the first times I made these tomatoes, the syrup formed by the butter and brown sugar came close to burning, so I added some water. The result was so good that now I always do it that way: let the sugar and butter caramelize a bit, then add about 2 tablespoons of water.

I don't feel contrite about putting this recipe into print. Anything this good shouldn't be kept secret. If I could get my hands on the entire book from that men's club and if the rest of the recipes turned out to be anywhere near as good as this one, I'd tell the world *all* its secrets.

Purée of Turnips

"Purée of turnips" should reach more people than "mashed turnips," I would think. The French have the proper respect for the turnip. Their *navets* are cooked with care and eaten with pleasure. Americans in general make horrid faces at the thought of having to eat this vegetable. Probably most of us have had encounters with watery, underseasoned mashes of turnip. Please do try this purée. I'll bet you'll like it, and afterwards, you may surprise yourself by yearning for it in moments when you are in need of succor.

2 medium-size white turnips (the kind with purple tops)
A good pinch of caraway seeds
2 or 3 tablespoons butter
1 teaspoon fresh basil, minced, or ½ teaspoon dried basil

1 slice bacon
2 minced scallions (optional)
Salt and pepper
A squeeze of lemon juice (optional)

Peel the turnips, cut them into quarters and then into thin slices. Put the turnip slices and the caraway seeds into a good-sized pot of boiling water and cook until almost tender, which may be in 10 minutes or in 20, depending on the age of your turnips, and on how thinly you've sliced them. Drain into a colander (this gets rid of any too-strong flavor) and give the turnip slices a quick rinse to get rid of the caraway seeds, unless you'd rather keep them. Add the butter, basil, bacon and, if you're using them, the scallions. Cook gently for a few minutes. Remove the bacon (chop and add it again later, if you like). Mash now—either a thorough puréeing or a gentle bashing with a fork. I've come to prefer the latter. Season to taste with salt and pepper and, perhaps, lemon juice.

The scallion, bacon and lemon juice are good with these turnips, either together or separately, but there are times you just don't feel like having them. At these times, the basil and butter give plenty of flavor, and you could even omit the basil. I wouldn't go so far as to leave out the butter, though!

Purée of Zucchini

This recipe was worked out the summer I first grew zucchini. There was just one little plant, or maybe it was one little hill. Anyway, it took over one whole end of my garden and seemed to grow several inches in all directions every day. It became known, fondly I think, as "The Monster," and it produced an awful lot of zucchini. It was quite a while after that summer before I could even think about zucchini, but then one day I found myself yearning for a big bowl of this, and it's been in my standard repertoire of foods-that-soothe ever since.

You can make it just as well with yellow or white summer squash, and perhaps best of all is a combination of squashes.

The cream at the end can be added or not according to your whim; it's good either way.

4 *small unpeeled zucchini, cut into small cubes*	2 *tablespoons butter*
	Salt and pepper
½ *small onion, minced, or 2 or 3 minced scallions*	2 *tablespoons heavy cream (optional)*
¼ *cup minced parsley*	

Just barely cover the zucchini and onion with water. Boil until the zucchini is thoroughly tender. Quickly boil off any water that remains, stirring so nothing will burn. (Or drain the water off if you don't mind losing a great deal of not only vitamins, but also taste.) Add the parsley, butter and salt and pepper; mash coarsely with a potato masher or a large spoon. Don't try to do this in the blender or you will have squash soup, although that's nice, too. Add the cream, if you're using it, and reheat if the purée has cooled off.

Serves 1 or 2.

You can eat this purée from a bowl with a spoon. It will have enough body, though, to be perfectly acceptable as a side dish for a dinner. Acceptable? It's delicious! I make a whole meal of it.

Tarragon Cream Salad Dressing

Another variation on the theme of sugar-on-lettuce, this happens to be one of the best salad dressings in the world. You start out by making a simple base, then adding a little sour cream when you use it. I have some in my icebox most of the time. (I still haven't learned to say "refrigerator," but I'm seriously thinking of beginning to say "fridge.")

1 egg	*¼ teaspoon dried tarragon*
¼ cup sugar	*Sour cream*
3 tablespoons tarragon vinegar	

Combine everything except the tarragon and sour cream in a blender container; whir briefly. Put into a small bowl that will fit over boiling water in one of your saucepans. (Or use a double boiler, but this sort of *bain-marie* arrangement works better for this small an amount.) Place over the boiling water and stir gently until the mixture begins to thicken. Remove from the source of heat. Add the tarragon. (This procedure takes very little time; it's not one of those booby-trap situations where "stir until thickened" finds you standing at the stove for 45 minutes.)

Keep the dressing under refrigeration. (How's that for a way around the icebox-refrigerator-fridge problem?) To use, combine a little of the tarragon mixture with sour cream. I use roughly half-and-half of each.

Serve with any sort of salad, but it's magnificent tossed with a simple bowl of torn-apart Boston, bibb or limestone lettuce.

I wish I knew more really unusual salad dressings like this, dressings unrelated to the usual French or mayonnaise types. If any of you know of one, would you send it on to me?

BREADS AND SANDWICHES

CRUNCHY FOODS—most of them, at any rate. Snappy, too, a lot of them. Good, all of them.

Of breads you make yourself, we have here five—Ola's Feathery Muffins, Snap Doodle (a coffee cake), popovers, pancakes and biscuits. Then there are a number of things to do *to* bread— French toast and a miscellany that includes some good ways to treat English muffins.

The sandwiches are guaranteed mood-lifters for me. Probably for you, too.

Biscuits

There's an old story about a Northern spy who was unmasked by a Southern family during the late unpleasantness between the states. The spy couldn't be faulted on Southern accent, graciousness, charm or seeming knowledge. He would have gotten away with his mission except for one thing: he flunked the biscuit test. In the course of dinner with the Southern family, biscuits were served—of course. The spy broke off pieces of biscuit, buttered them, ate them. "Aha!" said his hosts. "A spy!" A true Southerner, so the story goes, would have split each biscuit in two immediately, buttered the inside, then put the two halves back together so there would be a layer of melted butter inside. He would have treated biscuits with the reverence they deserve.

Here's a worthy biscuit, straight from the South.

1 cup flour	*½ teaspoon sugar (optional)*
2 teaspoons baking powder	*2½ tablespoons butter or lard*
¼ teaspoon salt	*⅓ cup plus 1 tablespoon milk*

Sift the dry ingredients together, or just mix them together if you're using presifted flour. Add the butter or lard with a pastry blender, 2 knives or those marvelous kitchen utensils, your 2 hands. Add the milk. Knead lightly on a floured board for just ½ minute or so. Roll out or pat with your hands till the dough is ½ inch thick. Cut with a biscuit cutter. Put the biscuits on a greased baking sheet and bake at 425° for 10 to 15 minutes, depending on their size. When eating, be sure to split and butter first, so you won't be yanked off to a prison camp.

Biscuit making is not my strong point, so sometimes I cheat and use Bisquick. I ignore the directions on the package, though, and do this:

2½ cups Bisquick	*1 tablespoon sugar*
3 tablespoons melted butter	*½ cup milk*

Mix all the ingredients together. Roll or pat out thicker than usual, about ¾ to 1 inch; cut. Bake at 350°.

Biscuits all by themselves can soothe away many a mood. Or eat them with soup or as part of any sort of meal.

Ola's Feathery Muffins

These muffins have everything going for them. They taste entirely different from any muffins you've ever tasted: that's the potato flour and the large amount of egg. They're the lightest muffins in the world: that's the high proportion of beaten egg white. They're the lowest in carbohydrates: whoever thought you'd be able to make a batch of muffins with only four table-spoons of flour? (And potato flour, at that, not wheat.) Try these when you feel a need for bread of some sort. Once you try them, it'll be specifically Ola's muffins you yearn for. They're the best.

2 *eggs, separated*
1 *teaspoon sugar*
A *dash of salt*
4 *tablespoons potato starch (look in the Kosher section of gro-*
cery stores, or get potato flour at a health food store)
¾ *teaspoon baking powder*
1 *tablespoon very cold water*

Beat the egg whites until stiff. Add the sugar and salt to the yolks and beat until well mixed; fold in the whites. Combine the potato starch and baking powder and mix well into the egg mixture. Stir in the cold water. Fill well-greased muffin pans ¾ full; bake at 450° for about 18 minutes. If you want little muffins, bake in "gem" pans for approximately 14 minutes. This recipe will make about 15 tiny muffins, 9 or 10 of the bigger ones.

And you'll eat 'em *all* up.

Candy's Pancakes

It was in the realm of cooking that some of the first strides (or tiptoes) toward equality for women took place, long before there was such a thing as a Women's Movement. But mostly in just two areas—outdoor cooking and, of all things, the making of pancakes.

It's easy to understand the appeal that outdoor cooking seems to have to men. Over a fire or glowing coals, they can have a nice atavistic trip back to being cave men. It's *muy macho*. But pancakes? Who knows. A lot of otherwise undomesticated males make them. One friend of mine, before she went off on a trip, had to insure that her husband wouldn't starve to death in her absence by giving him a course in how to warm up frozen dinners, a course that included a lesson in how to turn on the oven. And yet that same husband had been cooking pancakes for their Sunday night supper for years.

Be you male or female, making pancakes is rather fun—and eating them, a fine experience.

There are thin, crêpelike pancakes. And fat, flannelly Adirondack flapjack-type pancakes. And little silver dollar ones. And big dinner-plate-size ones. Suit your own inclination. Use the recipe below, but add more milk if, like me, you prefer thin pancakes. Or use a mix: there are excellent ones available at most health food stores.

1 cup milk or buttermilk	*1 teaspoon baking soda*
1 egg	*A dash of salt*
1 cup flour	*½ teaspoon sugar (optional)*

Mix everything together just until the dry ingredients are moistened. Cook on a hot griddle or skillet, turning once. (To tell if the griddle's hot enough, sprinkle a few drops of water on it. If the water bounces around, makes a lot of noise and evaporates almost immediately, the griddle's ready.)

This is my daughter Candy's recipe, and with it she makes delicious, tender pancakes for us and her friends. Tremendously soothing, especially for me, when they're delivered buttered and syruped to my bedside on a Sunday morning.

This amount makes six or seven 4-inch fat pancakes or quite a few more thin ones if you add more milk. If there's batter left over, it will keep well for a week or so in the refrigerator.

Snap Doodle

Katie, my older daughter, insists that this coffee cake appear in this book. I guess she's right. It *is* soothing, as well as being the best coffee cake in the world. Deachie, my grandmother, gave me the recipe a long time ago, and I think it was her own invention. At least, I've never run across it anywhere else, and she was the one under whose name it appeared in the *Iowa Centennial Cook Book,* put out in the 1940's.

4 or 5 tablespoons butter
½ cup sugar
1 egg, well beaten
1 cup milk
1½ scant cups sifted flour

2 tablespoons baking powder
3 or 4 tablespoons brown sugar
2 tablespoons chopped nuts, preferably pecans
½ teaspoon or so cinnamon

Cream two tablespoons of the butter with the sugar. Add the egg, milk, flour and baking powder. Mix well. Pour into a greased pan, about 10 x 10 inches.

Now the topping: Unlike the procedure in most coffee cakes, these topping ingredients are not mixed together. Sprinkle the brown sugar on top of the batter in the baking pan, and don't worry if there are lumps in the sugar; they'll just make it even better. Next, sprinkle on the chopped nuts, preferably pecans (if you'd rather, the nuts may be omitted without serious loss). Then shake on the cinnamon. (I add some nutmeg, too—just a little—or sometimes use a pre-mixed pumpkin pie spice.) Then, bit by bit, dab on dots of the remaining butter. This is the real secret of Snap Doodle: the little lumps of butter sink down through the batter as it cooks and carry the brown sugar, cinnamon and nuts with them, and you end up with small wells of flavor throughout the cake. Fantastic! (The large amount of baking powder helps, too. This is a light but rich concoction.)

Bake at 350° for 20 to 25 minutes, when it will be all brown and bubbly. Serve hot with butter. (You can make it ahead and reheat when wanted or even freeze it.)

This used to be—and maybe still is—served at mid-morning coffee parties in Iowa. I personally find it very helpful toward giving me the strength to read the *New York Times* on any given Sunday morning.

Lazyperson's Popovers

Can you imagine anyone not liking popovers? Not easily. Restaurant and home kitchen reputations have been built on them with little help from anything else. The way they puff up seems somewhat magical, and they taste so very good.

Part of all this excitement about popovers is because they're supposed to be so difficult—well, tiresome, at any rate—to make. Most books and most cooks tell you to beat, beat, beat the batter, then get popover pans red hot and so on and on. These popovers pop as well as the traditional ones, and taste just as good, but they're a cinch to make.

>   2 eggs   1 cup milk
>   1 cup flour   1 large pinch salt

Put all the ingredients into a bowl. Stir *gently* with a fork or spoon until the big lumps are gone. Little lumps—don't worry about them. Fill well-buttered custard cups about ⅔ full with batter. Put them into a cold oven; turn the heat to 450° and bake for half an hour. Then take out your gorgeous, brown, high-puffed popovers and eat them at once.

It's supposed to be important not to open the oven door while these are baking. I haven't tried opening it, so I don't know for sure. I *have* discovered, however, that the oven doesn't have to be cold when you put the popovers in; an already hot environment works just as well. Also, you can keep this batter on hand in your refrigerator for days on end in a jar or bowl and just make a popover or two whenever you feel like it.

You might try popovers if you, unlike most of us, are trying to gain weight. I've put on three pounds in the past two days, just testing these in one way and another.

Popovers with Maple Syrup

These come, like so many of my recipes and food prejudices, out of memories of my childhood. When I remember the days when I was a little girl, it's terribly apt to be some food experience that comes to mind. I guess I just always have liked to eat and have been surrounded for most of my life by people who felt the same way.

Someone, somewhere, sometime used to give me popovers with maple syrup, which seemed to me then—and still does— to be a marvelous treat.

> Make popovers the easy way (see page 147). Open the top of each one carefully and put butter and maple syrup down into the cavity inside.

That's all. Just eat with a knife and fork—and consider yourself lucky.

Bread and Butter and Sugar

Bread and butter and sugar is an absolute desperation move. It's for moments when you have to pick up some energy in a great hurry. You can make a piece of this in about ten seconds and carry it off with you.

It's just what it sounds like. You butter a piece of bread, then sprinkle it with sugar. The sugar gives you practically instant energy. The butter and bread maintain you for a while. It's somewhat the same idea as eggnog (see page 229), but more portable. Don't bother with a plate for it. Carry it in your hand— just be sure not to tip the sugar off!

It tastes very good, so good that I'm afraid to ever have it again, lest it become too much of a habit, as it's far from a diet food.

Cinnamon Toast

This is one of those things everyone knows how to make. But there are some especially good little tricks with cinnamon toast that you may not know about. Making toast, buttering it, then sprinkling it with cinnamon and sugar is only a beginning. Two other ways:

> Put the buttered, well-cinnamon-and-sugared toast on a cooky tin or other baking pan, then bake or broil it (watching closely so it won't burn) until the topping has melted. This is my favorite way with cinnamon toast.

> or

> A fancier way: Start with an unsliced loaf of bread. Cut it into 1-inch slices. Remove crusts. Cut each slice into 3 strips. Roll each strip around first in melted butter, then in a cinnamon and sugar mixture. (The strips should be thoroughly coated.) Put onto a rack over a pan so they'll cook on all sides. Bake at 400° for about 20 minutes. The coating will look melted and soft when you remove the strips from the oven, but it becomes harder and crunchy almost at once. (This is also true of the simpler version above.)

For either of these versions of cinnamon toast, try adding a little nutmeg to the cinnamon and sugar mixture, or perhaps some allspice or ground cloves or ginger or grated lemon peel. I always add nutmeg, and I think I'll try the others, too. Or maybe a lemon toast—it seems to me that you could combine sugar, lemon juice and grated lemon peel and have something quite wonderful.

Fried Bread

When you want a quick, crisp breakfast or snack, remember fried bread. You just take a piece of bread and fry it! In butter. It will drink up a lot of butter; if you want it to use less, dry the bread out in a slow oven or just use stale bread.

Serve to suit your particular mood . . . plain . . . or sprinkled with granulated or confectioner's sugar . . . or with jelly . . . or with butter or maple syrup . . . or beside eggs . . .

If you remove the crust of the bread before frying, you can call it a crouton, and you can serve any soft mixture—creamed chicken and ham (page 68), for instance—on it. Cut the bread in two diagonally or just into a circle before frying.

English Muffins Baked with Honey

There's another wonderful thing to do with English muffins instead of coating them with chocolate butter (see page 233). For breakfast, for instance, in case you have a silly prejudice against eating chocolate first thing in the morning. (I'll bet you wouldn't object to a cup of cocoa at that time of day.) But also when you just want something sweet and chewy and somewhat dry.

Split and toast English muffins and spread them with your usual amount of butter. Then add about 1 tea-

spoon of honey to each muffin half and spread it
around. Bake now at 325° or so for just a few minutes
until the honey and butter more or less disappear.
(Where they've gone is into every pore of the muffins.)
Eat them, but with caution. The muffins will be extremely hot.

This procedure is easy if you have a toaster-oven, but even
if you have to use a toaster *and* an oven, it's not much of a
problem.

French Toast, Plain or Fancy

They used to have not-bad food on the overnight trains (the
Century and the Commodore Vanderbilt) that ran between New
York and Chicago, or at least so it seemed to a little girl, Glenn
Hope Ellis, on her way to visit her grandparents. The breakfast
French toast was particularly exciting. It wasn't served with the
butter and maple syrup of home, but with confectioner's sugar
dusted on top and currant jelly on the side. Oh, my!

When I grew up I never lost my taste for French toast. Sometimes with maple syrup, sometimes with sugar and jelly. My
children have never taken to the sugar and jelly way, but then
they've never been on long distance trains. And as I grew older,
I also learned some of the many fancier-still versions of French
toast and the names other countries give to them.

The basic French toast: Beat together (I use a
blender) 1 egg and a little milk—maybe ¼ or ⅓ cup.
Pour it into a plate, and into this dip 1 or 2 pieces of
bread, cut in half if you like. Let the bread soak a while
in the liquid or cook it right then. Heat a little butter

in a frying pan or griddle until a few drops of water sprinkled on will sizzle. Then cook the bread over moderate heat until it's golden brown on both sides. Serve hot.

Variations, many of which make French toast more acceptable for non-breakfast times of day: Add a flavoring to the egg-milk mixture—vanilla extract, cinnamon, nutmeg, rum, grated lemon peel and so on. Or vary the liquid by using cream or water. (Water's surprisingly good in this.)

Use different breads. Just removing the crust before baking fancies things up. French or Italian bread makes superb French toast. Cracked wheat's good, also raisin bread. Date and nut bread should be delicious.

Try different toppings: Blueberry or other fruit syrups. Creamed chipped beef (which is on page 40). A light custard sauce alone or with sweetened fruit. Apple sauce (especially the homemade on page 193).

The French call their French toast *pain perdu,* "lost bread." The Germans have *arme ritter,* which I think I've read somewhere means "poor knights." I've even seen it called "Toast à la Duchesse" in one book published in America in 1907. I think I'll just go on calling it French toast. That's what the New York Central Railroad called it, when there was a New York Central Railroad.

Cucumber Sandwiches

The cucumber sandwich is just one more example of the joys of simplicity. Don't go gussying it up—all you need to make this cool, lovely treat are:

2 *slices bread (homemade or*   1 *cucumber, peeled and very*
    small-bakery)   *thinly sliced*
Mayonnaise   *Freshly ground black pepper (no*
                                            salt)

Spread both slices of bread with mayonnaise. On one piece put as many thin slices of cucumber as you can comfortably fit in. I make overlapping rows of them and usually manage about 15 slices—3 rows of 5 slices —on each sandwich. Grind fresh pepper over the cucumber and close the sandwich up. If possible, chill thoroughly before eating.

When I went to an office every day, I often used to take one of these sandwiches and a can of vegetable juice for my lunch. This meal made me feel calm, thin, chic and healthy—all highly desirable states of mind.

Liederkranz and Onion Sandwiches

A bar I used to go to in New York served only one sort of solid food: Liederkranz and onion sandwiches. That was all they needed to serve. A bunch of us, young and broke, spent happy hours there after work, drinking ten-cent draft beer and eating these thirty-five-cent sandwiches for dinner.

Use dark bread, very ripe Liederkranz and thinly sliced onion. Rye, pumpernickel or a whole-grain bread, a good chewy one, would be fine. The Liederkranz should be at room temperature and ripe to the point of runniness. I like to use mild red onion, but stronger souls may prefer more pungency. These same stronger souls might add mustard, too—a Düsseldorf, no doubt. The most I might add would be butter, spread on the bread, but why bother?

Maybe—just maybe—if you make these sandwiches at home, they'll still cost you thirty-five cents. Maybe not. But, nevertheless, they'll be something you're glad you know about, I would imagine. Perfect for when you want something simple and utterly down-to-earth. Not so good if you have plans for later that involve being with other people. You'll reek.

Peanut Butter Sandwiches

I recently borrowed a cookbook from my sister-in-law and found in it a slip of paper with a recipe in her handwriting. Here is what that fine cook had written.

"Take 2 slices bread from package. Take peanut butter from shelf. Open jar. Take knife. Spread peanut butter carefully on bread. Place slices together, being careful so that filling will be on inside—not outside—of sandwich. Serve on waxed paper so as not to use dish."

She claims she wrote it for her daughter years ago. Sure, Celeste. Anyway, it's a pretty good guide to the basic peanut butter sandwich. The first change most people would make after this beginning would be to toast the bread and to add jelly or jam. This (with or without toasting the bread) makes the PBJ, a staple without which many children would be unable to function. My daughter Candy seems to have a need for it at least once a day.

People go a little wacky about their peanut butter sandwiches once they leave the simple realm of the PBJ. Peanut butter and bacon is quite sensible, but I have actually known people who have occasional strong cravings for peanut butter and mayonnaise, peanut butter and Marshmallow Fluff and even peanut butter and brown sugar. I feel about those the way I suppose most people feel about my own two favorites, peanut butter and chutney and peanut butter, catsup and bacon, both of them open-faced and broiled or baked until hot and just beginning to brown. I've mentioned these in another book and had people say things like, "About that peanut butter, catsup and bacon sandwich, is it really edible?" *Edible!*—it's magnificent. Just plain peanut butter and catsup isn't bad, either.

Grilled Cheese Sandwiches

This is what my husband always says he's going to make himself for dinner when he feels that I'm tired or sick and shouldn't be cooking, or when he just can't stand the thought of anybody bending over a hot stove. The fact that he hasn't done it yet is only a testimony to my love for cooking. One of these days, I'll call his bluff.

He doesn't really say *"grilled* cheese"—just "cheese." But that sounds too unappetizing. He does have an occasional grilled cheese sandwich, but I make it. There are several good ways. Just three of these:

> *The classic:* A slice of Cheddar or American cheese between 2 slices of bread. Butter the outsides; cook fairly slowly on a grill or in a frying pan. (My favorite variation of this: a small blob of jelly in the middle of the cheese.)
> *With cheese spreads:* Pimiento cheese, in particular.

I had it for lunch at a drugstore every day for a year in college, in place of the dorm food my parents were paying for.

Open-face: Broiled or baked; not really grilled. Toast the bread first or just put it on a well-buttered pan. Use cheese alone or top with sliced tomato, slivered onion and/or partly cooked bacon.

But I think what my husband really has in mind when he makes his request for the cheese sandwich (maybe he really does *want* it, too) is two slices of bread with a pre-cut slice of processed yellow "flat cheese," as our ten-year-old calls it, between them. It's not for me, but . . .

Monte Cristo Sandwiches

The Count would have found his imprisonment more bearable if they had served him these sandwiches instead of just giving them the name when they were invented in this century.

I'll give you the more-or-less authentic and original version of the Monte Cristo, but you should know that it's made many other ways, too, and I'll tell you about some of them.

Make a 3-layer sandwich, buttering the insides of all 3 pieces of bread. The usual filling is thin slices of ham, chicken and Swiss cheese. Cut the sandwiches in two and pin each half with toothpicks so they won't fall apart. Dip in a French toast–type mixture (1 egg beaten with 2 or 3 tablespoons milk) and cook in butter until golden. Serve with currant jelly on the side.

Now the variations:

Use any other filling. Ham and cheese alone, for instance, is a basic one. Tongue would be good. Any cheese will do; Cheddar or Monterey Jack would probably be the best substitutes for Swiss.

Use only two slices of bread.

Serve with a sauce instead of jelly. A plain white or béchamel or one that has become a mornay by the addition of a little grated cheese. Or use something sweet other than currant jelly: plum jam, for example.

Add seasonings to the beaten egg and milk. A drop or two of Tabasco, a pinch of any herb, dry mustard, or a dash of any sort of seasoned salt or spice.

Bake instead of frying. Just put the sandwich in a small, well-buttered pan. Pour on the mixture of beaten egg and milk. Bake at 375° until the sandwich looks golden brown and beautiful, 10 or 15 minutes.

With all these possibilities, you should be able to make a Monte Cristo to fit almost any mood.

Mozzarella en Carrozza

Mozzarella en carrozza is more or less an Italian version of the grilled cheese sandwich. At least, the way I make it, and the way I'll be telling you about, certainly is. There's another way of doing it, probably more authentic, since it makes the name, which means, "Mozzarella cheese in a carriage," make sense. That way involves hollowing out hunks of bread until they look like bathtubs for doll houses. Pieces of cheese are tucked into the cavities in the bread; then there's dipping into flour, egg and flour again, and then deep-frying. Too much work—too hard to do properly. You're apt to end up with a crisp crust outside and cold cheese inside. *Lots* of Italians do it this way instead:

Use thin-sliced bread or cut ¼-inch slices of Italian bread; cut slices of Mozzarella the same thickness. Either remove the crusts and cut the pieces in half to make rectangles or use a fairly large cookie cutter to make circles of bread and cheese. Make into sandwiches. Soak in beaten egg for 15 minutes or more, turning once. Cook in a frying pan in oil (olive oil, if possible) till puffed and golden brown on both sides.

Serve, if you like, with an anchovy sauce made by cooking 4 flat anchovies in 4 tablespoons of butter until they disappear (if you can believe it). Use the sauce hot if you're going to use it at all. I wouldn't think of doing such a thing myself. A slight sprinkle of salt does nicely instead. A tomato sauce, perhaps, should be good.

If you don't want to wait while your little sandwiches soak up egg for 15 minutes, just dip them (edges, too) in flour first, then in egg; they can then be fried right away.

Try very small ones for appetizers: cut them out with a tiny cookie or biscuit cutter. Also, if you don't mind a little culinary heresy, try making them with Monterey Jack cheese on which you've put just a little taco sauce or one of the milder hot pepper sauces—Frank's Louisiana Red Hot Sauce, for example.

DESSERTS

LOTS OF PEOPLE are cheered by *any* dessert; their only requirement is that it be sweet. But then, there are the fruit freaks, the chocolate people and those for whom you practically have to keep an intravenous injection of ice cream going. So you'll find all these here, plus a few cookies, several representatives of the custard and pudding group—magnificent soothers—and a few offbeat suggestions such as snow candy and cream puffs with wine.

To a large group of sweet-lovers, eggnogs and milkshakes are the super-treats. You'll find them in the chapter on Odds and Ends.

Chocolate Bread Pudding

Chocolate bread pudding! As you will have gathered if you have read the introduction to this book, I go into ecstasies over it. It all goes back (as do so many of everyone's most soothing foods) to childhood experience. It seems incredible now, but in my family we used to have dessert every night (soup, too). More incredible, we were all fairly thin in those days. There certainly wasn't any question about my favorite of all those gorgeous desserts—chocolate bread pudding with hard sauce won in a walk.

3 squares (3 ounces) unsweetened chocolate	2 cups bread cubes
1 cup sugar	2 tablespoons butter
4 cups milk	½ teaspoon vanilla

Put the chocolate, sugar and milk into a pan and heat until the chocolate is melted and the milk scalded. Add the bread cubes, butter and vanilla. Pour into a buttered casserole. Bake for 1 hour at 350°.

Note that there are no eggs in this recipe, and unlike most recipes for chocolate bread pudding, you don't have to place the casserole in a pan of hot water for the baking. Also, you don't have to crumb the bread; the cubes of bread just disappear. These are three of the things that make this such a satisfactory recipe. The fourth is that it's delicious.

These amounts of ingredients make a great deal of chocolate bread pudding, and you may want to cut them down to half or even a quarter. I'm giving it this way because of that dream meal I'm going to have someday: this much chocolate bread pudding, all to myself. As a dessert, it will serve 4.

I guess I'd better tell you about the hard sauce, too. It's an integral part of chocolate bread pudding.

Hard Sauce

The fitting finish not only for chocolate bread pudding, but also for Christmas plum pudding or any other hot dessert. Not bad just by itself, either.

4 tablespoons butter	*1 teaspoon vanilla*
1 cup confectioner's sugar	*A few drops of water or milk*

Soften the butter a bit by beating it, by hand or by machine. Add the sugar, a tablespoon or two at a time, alternately with a drop or two of vanilla. When the va-nilla is used up, switch to the water or milk. When all the ingredients are in, you will have a soft sauce; it will thicken up as it chills. Put it onto a pretty little plate and swirl a design into the top with the tines of a fork. Chill for at least an hour or two.

Serve cold to put onto the hot pudding. It will melt into the most delightful pools of flavor you ever tasted.

Chocolate Mousse

Chocolate mousse has a lot going for it. Smoothness, richness, chocolateness, luxuriance and connotations of "now-you're-eat-ing-one-of-the-best-things-in-the-world." To make it the easy way:

1 small package (6 ounces) choc-olate bits (or 6 ounces semi-sweet chocolate, broken into small pieces)	*A dash of cinnamon*
	5 tablespoons boiling water
	4 eggs, separated
	2 tablespoons brandy or rum

Put the chocolate and cinnamon into a blender, add the boiling water and immediately blend until the chocolate is melted, which will be almost immediately. Add the egg yolks and brandy or rum and blend until they're all combined, stopping the motor and scraping down the sides as needed. With the blender running, add the egg whites and continue to blend until the color of the mixture is uniform. Again, you may have to stop the machine and scrape down any darker-colored mixture on the sides. Pour into a decorative bowl and refrigerate for several hours. The mousse will be edible—highly edible—in an hour, but it's at its best after at least 4 hours of chilling. By the way, don't be alarmed if the mixture is very thin before being chilled; it's supposed to be.

Without a blender, the mousse isn't quite as simple, but it's still well worth the trouble. Melt the chocolate in a double boiler with the cinnamon and water. Beat the egg yolks well and add them, along with the brandy or rum. Then beat the egg whites to the good old stiff-but-not-dry stage, beat in ¼ of them, then fold the rest in as you would when making a soufflé.

This mousse is a lovely thing to have on hand in the refrigerator for idle moments of vague unease or for a meal when the mood strikes. It's a fine breakfast for a day that would be otherwise grim, but in that case you surely wouldn't want the brandy or rum, since the mousse is not cooked at all and the full alcohol content remains. So if you want mousse for breakfast or if for other reasons you don't choose to include alcohol, just add extra water and a teaspoon of flavoring—vanilla or perhaps rum or brandy extract—where the recipe indicates brandy or rum. This will give you the original flavor without the kick. (But believe me, it's a very small kick indeed, unless you eat the whole mousse all by yourself at one sitting, which people have been known to do.)

The proportions of the recipe work out well, in fact, for one person. When I make it to serve to a dinner party of eight, though, or even just for four of us, I always double the recipe. Theoretically, that's a great deal too much, but I've never had any left over yet. If you want it to go farther, chill the mousse in little individual cups.

Suzanne's Fudge Bars

Suzanne is Suzanne Dickson, my godmother. Her fudge bars are perfection, and about the most chocolaty things around. When you feel you can't live without a heavy dose of chocolate, try these.

When I wrote Suzanne to ask if I could use this recipe, which I've cherished for years, she wrote back, "I am still trying to find a successful recipe. The success of it was that you probably remember them and our kitchen with nostalgia." Probably that *is* part of it—that wonderful, warm kitchen and that wonderful, warm godmother. But quite aside from that, this is a *highly* successful fudge bar, no matter what Suzanne may say.

Here's how I learned to make fudge bars long years ago in one of the two happiest kitchens in Mount Pleasant, Iowa. (The other one was my grandmother's.)

4 ounces chocolate (dark, bitter)	*¼ teaspoon vanilla*
1 to 2 sticks butter	*2 cups sugar*
2 eggs	*1 cup flour*

Melt the chocolate and butter together. Cool, then add the unbeaten eggs and vanilla. To this, gradually add the sugar and flour.

Pat out ½ inch thick in a buttered pan, 9 x 5 inches. Bake at 350° for 10 to 15 minutes, or until the top is crusty and the insides still gooey. Cut while warm.

About that wide range in the amount of butter. I originally wrote down, in Suzanne's kitchen, "One-half pound of butter," but that makes a fudge bar that, while tasting marvelous, does perhaps have a bit too much butter oozing out. I may have meant to write "one-half cup." Who knows? (And Suzanne seems to have abandoned her fudge bars, so I can't ask her.) At any rate, I've tried using five ounces of butter—a stick and a quarter— and the fudge bars are fine. So do as you like.

I also wrote down, "Can add one cup nuts." That would un-doubtedly be good, though I really haven't tried it that way. And, further, I wrote down, "Best next day." What a lot of nonsense *that* is! How could anyone ever have any left for the next day to find out?

Cream Puffs and Wine

If your idea of being soothed is to sink into the most utter luxury imaginable, try cream puffs and wine. Not just any cream puffs, though. They should be lightly nutmeg-flavored, filled with *crème Chantilly,* a lightly sweetened whipped cream, and topped with a dark but not bitter chocolate frosting. And the wine ideally should be Chateau d'Yquem, that fruity, heady, blissful nectar of a *sauternes*. Just thinking of this combination can, once you've tried it, make you smile softly to yourself and go into a happy trance.

The quantities given will make two large cream puffs. Eat them yourself or share this moment of Lucullan bliss with someone you are very fond of. Two of you can finish off the bottle of wine, too, no matter how slowly and tranquilly you sip.

The puffs: Combine 2 tablespoons of butter and ¼ cup plus 1 tablespoon of water in a saucepan. Boil until the butter is melted; remove from the fire and add, all at once, a mixture of ¼ cup of flour and a pinch each of sugar, salt and nutmeg. Stir until the dough forms a cohesive ball; 2 or 3 minues will do it. Then beat in 1 unbeaten egg. (To make twice as many, double all the ingredients except the water—make that ½ cup—and add the eggs one at a time.) Make 2 rounded mounds on a greased baking sheet and cook at 400° until the puffs are a soft, golden brown, about 25 minutes. Remove from the oven and immediately either make a good-sized slit in the side of each one or cut them in half horizontally. If you leave out this step, the puffs will be soggy and you might as well forget the whole thing. These puffs, unfilled, can be frozen, by the way. Just warm them a little, then let them cool again before filling.

The cream: When the puffs are cool, make the *crème Chantilly* by beating heavy cream until it's only moderately stiff but not dry at all. One quarter-cup of cream will be enough for your 2 cream puffs, but not all mixers will whip that small an amount, so do what you can—use a wire whisk, for instance. Add just a few drops of vanilla and 2 teaspoons of powdered sugar. Fill the puffs.

The frosting: The easiest and best frosting—exactly right for these cream puffs—is the simple combination of ¼ of a 6-ounce package of semi-chocolate pieces, melted, mixed with 2 tablespoons of sour cream.

The wine: As I said above, Chateau d'Yquem is the very thing here. However, paying for it can be traumatic, so use another *sauternes* or any dessert wine you like, though I think cream sherry, for instance, would be too sweet and heavy. Half the joy of this combination is in the chilly clarity of the wine.

Milk Rice

"Milk rice," said a friend. "That's what I remember out of my childhood, being fed something called milk rice." Rice **pudding?** "No, just milk rice; it's different, simple and very soothing." And so it is.

¼ *cup raw rice*	*A few grains of salt*
1½ cups milk	*½ teaspoon vanilla (optional)*
1 teaspoon butter	

Combine the rice and milk in the top of a double boiler and cook, covered, for 1 hour, stirring every 10 or 15 minutes. Before serving, mix in the butter and salt and vanilla if you're using it. Eat out of a bowl with cinnamon and sugar to sprinkle on at will (or brown sugar if spice doesn't appeal at the moment) and perhaps a jug of milk to pour on, too.

Quite a long way from rice pudding, as a matter of fact. Closer to a hot cereal. It's easy to see how a dish such as this would bring back memories of childhood cosseting. Incidentally, this was made for my friend by a Russian housekeeper (a mad

Russian, she says), but it's an old American custom that goes way, way back, and it's probably been made all over the world, wherever people need taking care of—and that's everywhere, for sure.

Rice Pudding

Milk rice, above, is all very well for those who were brought up on it, but for most of the rest of us, rice pudding is the real thing to calm the jangled nerve. Here's how to make it the good, old-fashioned honest way.

3 cups milk
⅓ cup uncooked rice
⅓ cup sugar
½ teaspoon vanilla

2 tablespoons dried currants or
  raisins (optional)
A dash of cinnamon (optional)

Combine all the ingredients and put them into a buttered baking dish. Bake at 300° for about 2¼ hours, or until the pudding has thickened, the rice is tender and the top is lightly browning.
Cool—or don't. Serve with cream—whipped or not.

And plan ahead: this is no last-minute treat. There's very little work involved, but a lot of time.

Ice Cream and Various Sundaes

The only way I can keep certain members of my family from practically drowning themselves in ice cream is not to have it in the house at all. And that's not very nice. So there's usually a half-gallon (at least) in our freezer, and sometimes a new one every day. Ice cream seems to certain people to go right to the heart of their problems and to smooth things out (or possibly to numb them).

Plain vanilla is my husband's favorite; you have to really love ice cream to feel this way. My friend Jane Heimlich taught me an old song about it, something about "Vanilla, dear, I hear you calling me." For me, chocolate sauce (page 191) or crushed, sweetened strawberries transform a blah food such I consider this to be into a feast. Whipped cream on top helps, too.

Have sundae makings on hand for times when the ice cream urge strikes. Chocolate sauce in the refrigerator and heavy cream ready to whip. Nuts in the freezer. Fruit to crush or interesting things like ginger marmalade to streak through your plain vanilla. The thought of my own favorite sundae would turn most people as green as it is itself—lime sherbert topped with chocolate sauce and whipped cream (don't sneer until you try it)— so whatever you dream up, don't be bashful about it.

My daughter Candy recently asked me why she couldn't have ice cream for breakfast. I thought about it and couldn't see why she shouldn't. There's milk in it and, in certain brands, eggs and often fruit—not too bad a breakfast. If it suits an occasional mood of hers and keeps her from totally turning against breakfast, she might as well have it.

Syllabub

An old recipe I've seen for syllabub calls for mixing certain ingredients in a bowl, then going out to the cowshed and milking the cow directly into the bowl. This was supposed to give the syllabub a frothiness that couldn't be gotten any other way, but it does seem rather impractical for most of us nowadays. We'll just have to make do with a beater or a whisk—*anything* rather than forgo syllabub, one of the nicest, simplest and most elegant of all desserts.

> If you don't have a cow: Beat together 1 cup of heavy cream, ½ cup of sugar, ¼ cup of not-too-dry sherry and the juice and grated peel of 1 lemon. (The grated peel is optional; I like it.) This can be done with an electric mixer, by hand with a whisk or even in a blender if you're careful not to let it run too long. The mixture should be as frothy as though you had a cow. Serve now or chill for a while. Serve if you wish, with lady fingers or any simple wafer-type cookie.

The origin of syllabub seems to be English, but it came to America in the early days of the colonies. Then, when America became temperance-minded, syllabub disappeared from cookbooks. Now, when we blithely throw wine, brandy and rum into half of the things we cook, it's a shame that we haven't rediscovered the only-mildly-alcoholic syllabub. I recommend it to you highly.

Crème Brûlée

At one point in their lives, my mother and father decided to become "gentlemen farmers," with a sampling of every possible sort of farm animal. Naturally these included some laying hens and a Jersey cow. "Mmm," said Mother, "just think of all the *crème brûlée* we can have!" This great luxury became a frequent treat for us, and we needed its touch of soothing elegance to repair the ravages of the grueling peon labor we were doing. Being gentlemen farmers with inadequate help isn't so very gentlemanly, or ladylike. It can get downright grubby. *Crème brûlée* reminded us that there still were other ways of life.

4 egg yolks	*1 teaspoon vanilla*
2 cups heavy cream	*Light brown sugar*
4 teaspoons sugar	

Beat the egg yolks thoroughly. Combine the cream and sugar in a saucepan and bring them to a boil. Immediately pour them in a very thin stream, stirring constantly, into the egg yolks. (This, including the beating of the egg yolks, can be nicely done in a blender.) Return to the saucepan and cook over a very low fire, stirring unceasingly, until the mixture is steaming hot and almost boiling. Add the vanilla. Pour into a well-buttered baking dish. Chill thoroughly.

When the custard (for that's what you've made) is completely cool, put a layer of brown sugar about ⅓ inch thick on top of it. Put under a broiler until the brown sugar melts, but watch this proceeding carefully, since brown sugar burns easily, which you *don't* want. You can eat the *crème brûlée* now or chill it again first. I prefer to chill it, since that makes the topping very crackly.

A purist version of *crème brûlée:* omit the sugar and vanilla in the custard. This way's good, too—the brown sugar top provides enough sweetness.

A compromise version for emergencies: make packaged vanilla pudding; chill. Top with brown sugar and continue as above. To make this better, add an egg yolk and a little vanilla to the pudding.

Floating Island

One of the happiest moments of my culinary life came when
I learned that Floating Island—dear, *sweet* Floating Island of
childhood memory—is exactly the same thing as *oeufs à la neige,*
a French dessert considered quite an epicurean treat. It was like
learning that an old dress you loved too much to throw away
is suddenly the height of fashion. I think the next time I need
soothing all the way down to my toes, I'll have a huge bowl of
Floating Island all to myself.

First make the custard base:

4 egg yolks (use "large" eggs)	*5 tablespoons sugar*
2 cups milk	*1 teaspoon vanilla*

Combine the egg yolks, milk and sugar by beating in a
mixer or blender. (Scald the milk first, if you like; it
does speed things up, but isn't necessary with pasteur-
ized milk.) Cook, stirring, over a very low fire or over
hot water until the custard thickens somewhat, coats a
silver spoon and is getting close to coming to a simmer.
Cool somewhat, stirring occasionally, then add the vanilla. Strain into a serving bowl or individual dishes;
chill.

Now the meringue:

4 egg whites
¾ cup granulated sugar

Beat the egg whites until they are foamy; then very
gradually, while still beating, add the sugar. Beat until

very stiff. Drop by large rounded spoonfuls into a large skillet filled with at least 2 inches of simmering water. Poach for 2 minutes on the first side. Turn—I find 2 large spoons work best for this—and poach for another 2 minutes. Remove to paper towels to drain, then place on top of custard.

Poach the meringue eggs in the milk you're going to use for the custard, if you want. Use vanilla bean instead of vanilla extract for an even finer custard (a 1-inch piece cooked with the mixture from the beginning, then removed).

This recipe theoretically serves 4 people. You could probably cut it in half, but I never have—why make a *little* Floating Island?

Some recipes for Floating Island specify a layer of fruit or broken-up cake or macaroons at the bottom or a layer of jelly in there somewhere. Do that if you like, but the recipe as I have given it is what I—and most of the French—think of as right.

"Boiled" Custard

"Boiled" has to be in quotation marks in the title of this recipe because, as in "boiled" eggs and "boiled" dressing for salad, the surest way to ruin it is to boil it. How these things came to be called "boiled" is a culinary mystery. Since we need all the mystery we can get in life, let's keep the old names with all their confusion.

Because of its softness, "boiled" custard is usually used as a sauce for puddings, gelatines, fruit and simple cakes, but a whole bowlful of it, unadorned and unadorning, is fantastically good. Just eat with a spoon and glow.

To make it, follow the instructions given for the custard base in Floating Island, the previous recipe. While you're at it, you might consider continuing right on with the rest of that recipe—but plain boiled custard is for the simpler moments in your life.

I don't usually think much of packaged puddings and sauces, but there's an English custard sauce mix that's really quite good. It's called Bird's Dessert Powder, and you can find it in many delicacy stores and even supermarkets. It's handy to have on hand when you *have* to have some boiled custard, but are short on eggs or time or energy. And incidentally, eggs don't seem to be listed among its ingredients at all. Wonder how they manage that?

Baked Custard

There was a time in my life when you'd just wind me up and I'd make baked custard, a double recipe, every day. That and vitamin pills can keep you going for a long time. Baked custard is just about as soothing as a food can be. After all, what is it but cooked eggnog? Incidentally, it makes a fine breakfast.

3 eggs	⅓ cup sugar
2 cups milk	1 teaspoon vanilla

If you have a blender, custard can be ready for the oven in about a minute, starting from scratch. Blend everything together briefly. Pour the mixture into 1 or 2 buttered baking dishes or 4 or 5 individual custard cups, then place them in a pan half-full of hot water. Bake at 325° for about 1 hour, or until when you stick a table knife into the center of the custard it comes out clean. (Or until when you gently shake the custard dish, the whole mass quivers all together cohesively.) Let it cool a bit at room temperature, then chill.

If you don't have a blender, go out and buy one. Or combine the milk and sugar; then slowly, while beating away, pour them over the eggs, which you have already beaten. Add the vanilla, then continue as above. You'd be better off with a blender.

Serves 1 to 4.

If you have a family, you might try keeping baked custard on hand all the time, as much a staple in your refrigerator as butter or cottage cheese. Someone's bound to need soothing almost every day.

Flan, or Caramel Custard

The Spanish add a caramel touch to their baked custard and call it *flan,* and adore it. The French do the same thing, but call it *crème renversée au caramel.* It's too sweet for me (and I definitely have a sweet tooth), but it seems as though the moods of a lot of people would get totally out of control without an occasional binge of it.

It's easy enough to make. Simply combine ½ cup of white sugar with 2 tablespoons of water and cook them together until they caramelize (form a brown syrup). Pour this into the bottom of the baking dish you plan to use or divide it between custard cups. On top of this, put the mixture for baked custard from the previous recipe, and cook as directed there; cool.

When you're ready to eat the *flan*, run a knife around the inside of the mold or custard cups, then invert onto a plate. The custard will plop out and the caramel run down its sides. The general visual effect will be of a rather well-behaved volcano.

Constantia Apple-Rum Flower

When you get right down to it, Constantia Apple-Rum Flower is just a glorified baked apple. But *how* it is glorified! An informal party dessert or a personal treat, for self-cosseting.

1 large apple, preferably a Golden Delicious
1 teaspoon sugar
½ teaspoon lemon juice
¼ teaspoon lemon peel, grated

½ teaspoon butter
1 teaspoon apricot or other jam or jelly
1 teaspoon rum

Use any tasty apple, but a Golden Delicious is especially good (and pretty) in this. Core most of the way to the bottom. Score the top of the apple rather deeply into sixths, right through the peel, so that the apple will open like a flower as it bakes. Place in an ovenproof serving dish big enough to allow the "petals" to open. Cover the bottom of the dish with 2 or 3 tablespoons of water. Put the sugar into the apple's cavity, then the lemon juice and grated lemon peel. Dot with small pieces of butter and the jam or jelly. (Experiment here, if you want—quince jelly, for example, does nicely.) Pour on the rum. Bake at 350° until tender, ¾ to 1 hour. Serve hot, warm or cold with a custard sauce (there's one on page 173).
Serves 1.

Increase the rum, if you want, or try an orange-flavored liqueur. Either way, though, you'll lose some of the delicacy of this charming flower.

Cider Gelatine

If you make this with fresh, unpasteurized, unpreserved cider, and especially if the cider is made from unsprayed apples, you will have a very pure thing indeed. If you can't find this sort of cider, there's a good, old-fashioned kind you can buy (Seneca) that's concentrated and frozen. But even if you're stuck with the usual blah cider, this is a good bet (though it might be wise to add a little lemon juice).

> Boil down 2 cups of cider to 1½ to 1¾ cups. (This will concentrate the flavor.) To this, add 1 packet of gelatine dissolved in ¼ cup of cold water. Stir well. Pour into a wet mold. Chill until set.
> Serves 2 to 4.

No sugar, no spice. Just lovely cider, turned into a dessert.

Lemon Gelatine

One friend of mine finds this the most soothing and cheering of foods. I think she makes it with a packaged mix though. She might enjoy the pureness of this gelatine even more. Both kinds sparkle and require little effort to make and practically no effort at all to eat.

Juice of 2 lemons, strained   *1 packet gelatine*
½ cup sugar   *Grated lemon peel (optional)*
Water

Combine the lemon juice and sugar in a measuring cup. Add enough cold water to bring the total up to 1½ cups. Then put ½ cup of plain cold water in a saucepan and sprinkle the gelatine on it. Stir over low heat until the gelatine is completely dissolved. When you can't see any trace of gelatine, add the lemon juice-sugar-water mixture and the lemon peel, if you're using it, and stir until everything's thoroughly combined. Pour into a mold. (Wet the mold first if you want to be able to unmold it.) Chill until set.

Lemon gelatine made this way won't be as yellow as the packaged mix kind, but it will look, taste and *be* much more real.

Broiled Fruit with Honey

Any fresh fruit—or, as a matter of fact, any canned fruit—tastes wonderful when broiled with honey. You've probably had grapefruit halves done this way, but have you had slices of orange drizzled with honey and put under the broiler until they're slightly browned? Or strawberries done the same way? Or canned pears? Broil the fruit right in the same dish you plan to serve it in. Eat as a whole meal for yourself or serve with breakfast or as a first course or dessert or side dish with meat for dinner. No food could be much more versatile than that, could it?

Strawberry Shortcake

The kind with biscuit-shortcake, the *real* kind. But if you're a fan of the spongecake variety of shortcake, go ahead and make it that way. Then, however, you won't know the bliss of the strawberry juices and the whipped cream sneaking into and softening parts of the shortcake while other parts stay firm and crisp in contrast.

Make a whole soup plate full of shortcake—why not? If a mood has driven you to have shortcake at all, you might as well give in to it all the way.

For the shortcake part, follow the instructions for biscuits on page 142, but increase the amount of sugar to 1 tablespoon and for a truly devastating shortcake, use cream instead of milk and use close to ½ cup of it. Roll out 1 inch thick and cut with a large cutter, about 3 inches in diameter, or around a saucer.

When the shortcakes are fresh from the oven, split them and butter the insides.

To serve, put the bottom half of each shortcake on a plate or in a soup plate. Cover it with sweetened, crushed strawberries, as much as you like. (Crush and sugar the strawberries at least 1 or 2 hours in advance, so a beautiful juice will have time to develop, or use thawed frozen sliced strawberries.) Put the tops of the biscuits in place. Top, if you want, with more strawberries, then a great glob of fairly soft whipped cream, sweetened or not. If you can, save one huge whole strawberry to set onto the top of the whipped cream.

Serves 2 to 4.

This strawberry shortcake should help you get rid of most bad moods. Unfortunately, though, you may be plunged back into depression when you read your bathroom scale a day or two later.

Blueberry Crisp

Some people go bananas over blueberries. My daughter Candy is one of these. When things in life make her unhappy, I can generally make her her usual glowing self again with a blueberry *anything*. She really prefers a pie, but that's hard work, so she is willing to settle for blueberry muffins, cake or pancakes. Or this easy-to-fix and delicious Blueberry Crisp. She didn't think it sounded very promising when I first proposed making it, but now she has thoroughly come around to it. I originally made it in a pie pan (a pretty brown ceramic one) to make her take more kindly to it, but in that case, all the ingredients have to be doubled.

Combine 2 cups of blueberries with 1 teaspoon of lemon juice and ¼ cup of sugar. (The frozen organically grown wild blueberries available in some health food stores are great for this.) Put them into a buttered 6- or 7-inch ovenproof pan (a small skillet, for instance).

Combine ¾ cup of brown sugar, ¾ cup of flour and 6 tablespoons of butter by mixing them with your fingers or a pastry blender. Crumble over the blueberries. Dot with 1 tablespoon of butter, in little pieces. Bake at 450° for about 20 minutes, or until the topping is lightly browning.

Serves 2 to 4.

Eat fresh from the oven or cooled or refrigerated, plain or with cream or ice cream. It's hard to tell from a pie, really. I should never have told Candy it was anything else.

German Apple Pancake

"Apple pancakes remind me of my mother's love," said a friend, and from the look on her face, I knew she really meant it. She didn't have her mother's recipe, so I searched in various books. No luck. Then, when I'd about given up, I happened to come across this German Apple Pancake in the first cooking notebook my own mother kept when she was a new bride.

It's a large, puffy, somewhat popoverlike pancake, with the apples cooked right in it, and it's fabulous. It's extremely similar to another "pancake" that I've been making with some regularity for the past few years. Just use one egg less and delete the apples and you have the other one, and it's a wonder, too.

3 eggs	*4 tablespoons butter*
½ cup milk	*2 to 3 tablespoons confectioner's*
½ cup flour	*sugar*
1 large apple	*Juice of ½ lemon*

Combine the eggs, milk and flour by buzzing in the blender, scraping down the sides of the container if necessary. (Mother's recipe, of course, has you do the beating by hand, since they didn't have blenders then.)

Peel and slice the apple. Cook the slices in the butter in a fairly large skillet until they are soft but not brown. (At least, that's what I do; the original recipe doesn't say.) Tip the pan around so the sides are coated with butter; with the pan still hot, pour in the egg mixture.

Put in the oven and bake 425° for 15 minutes. Then sprinkle with the confectioner's sugar and lemon juice. Return to the oven for a few minutes to glaze. Serve hot.

This makes a lot, enough to serve three or four, but it can be reheated. Cutting it down might present problems, but do try if you're feeling adventurous.

Pears and Provolone

Just a thought—you don't really have to know any more than the title, "Pears and Provolone." This combination is very Italian (I think) and very elegant (I know). But for more detail:

The pears should be ripe, melting and sweet. (If you're lucky enough to have someone send you some of those beautiful pears from Harry and David's in Medford, Oregon, this would be a good thing to do with them. I haven't tasted one of these in at least ten years, but I'll never forget how fantastic the few I've had were.)

The cheese: go to a good cheese shop and tell them your problem. You want a little fresh, soft, extra-fine *provolone* to eat with fruit. Or perhaps a *pecorino,* if it is available.

If possible, the pears should be cold and the cheese at room temperature.

My way of eating this is to put a pear and some slices of cheese on one of the prettiest dessert plates I can find. Then, with a fruit knife, I cut the pear into small pieces, peel each one as I go and—with fork or fingers—eat a little cheese with each piece of pear. And all the while I'm slowly sipping a glass of white wine. (Italian wine, naturally—Orvieto or Soave, for instance.)

Ola's Deep-Dish Apple Pie

No wonder I ate my dinner all up, most of the time, when I was young. There were things like Ola's deep-dish apple pie waiting to be eaten afterwards.

When I started cooking on my own, I read and tried various apple pie recipes. None of them had what Ola's did: lovely pure flavor; apples floating in a clear amber syrup. Finally I asked Ola, who was still cooking for my family, what she put into hers. "Apples," it turned out, "and butter and sugar." No cinnamon, no lemon juice—nothing at all to change the simple taste of the apples. Just sugar to sweeten—Ola used tart apples—and butter to enrich. I'll bet she did add one more thing, though—a pinch of salt. Ola always told me that to bring out flavor, you should add a little salt to anything sweet and a little sugar to anything salty.

> To make enough deep-dish pie to serve one or two (one for a whole meal), use a small casserole. The ovenproof glass dessert bowls that hold 1½ cups when filled to the brim will do, though something a little bigger will do even better.
>
> Peel tart cooking apples, slice them and fill the cooking dish with them. Then add sugar; just pour it on until it fills every nook and cranny. Use more than you think you could possibly need. (How do you like that for precise instructions? But "how much" sugar depends on the size of your dish and the tartness of the apples.) The butter goes next; again, more than you'd think. Ola used to plop hefty slices of it all over everything until you could hardly see the apples and sugar. Now sprinkle on just a little salt. Crust next (page

231), over the top and finely pinched at the edges to anchor it to the dish. Half the amount for a regular 8- or 9-inch pie shell should be about right.

Bake at 450° for 10 minutes, then at 350° for half an hour more, or until the crust is light brown and, if you're using a glass baking dish, you can see somewhat translucent apples in clear syrup.

Eat while it's still hot. If you like, serve with heavy cream, possibly whipped, or with vanilla ice cream. It doesn't need them, though. It's perfection just as is, and one of the great tranquility creators.

Fried Peach Pies

Fried peach pies are for times when you feel strongly enough about wanting to indulge yourself in this particular way to go to quite a bit of work for it. Or better yet, if you can get someone else to make them for you, you can *really* be calmed. They make the nicest Sunday morning breakfast there could ever be. They're small; you can probably eat two.

Ideally, the fried peach pie starts out with dried peaches, which you soak, sugar and stew. But try and find them. (I understand there are dried peaches around, but never when and where I'm looking for them.) I've been yearning for some of these pies off and on for ten years or so, so now I've worked out a compromise.

Dried or canned peaches	*Fat for deep-frying*
Granulated sugar	*Confectioner's sugar*
Pie crust (see page 231)	

If you have the dried peaches, follow the box instructions for soaking, sweetening and stewing. Then purée them in a blender or food mill. The purée should be as thick as oatmeal. If it isn't, cook it down a little. If dried peaches aren't available, drain canned ones, purée and sugar them and cook them down. You might add a little lemon juice to them, too. Amounts? Well, to make two little pies, I've used a buffet-sized can of peaches and 1½ tablespoons of sugar. You could probably also use baby food peaches, cooked down somewhat to make them thicker. If you use dried peaches, ¼ pound should be ample.

Now the pie crust: For 2 pies, or 3 if you roll quite thin, you'll need enough crust for a single-crust regular 8- or 9-inch pie. (See page 231.)

For each pie, roll a circle about the size of a saucer. Put a spoonful of peach purée in the middle and fold the crust over to make a turnover. Crimp the edges together very thoroughly by pressing down on them with the tines of a fork; then turn the pie over and repeat on the other side. If either you or the pies are limp from all this, put them in the refrigerator while they—or you—firm up a bit.

Then deep-fry at about 375° until they're light brown; drain. Sprinkle with confectioner's sugar. Eat while hot.

I've led you by the hand through this procedure to the point where it sounds much more difficult than it is, just because I love these so and want you to do them right. Perhaps I should just have said: "Make turnovers with a filling of sweetened peach purée. Deep-fry. Sprinkle with confectioner's sugar." Oh, well.

Don't try these with other fruits until you've tried them with peaches, and then you won't want to. You'll just want to keep eating fried peach pies over and over again.

Apple Tapioca, or Fish Eyes and Glue

Don't let the fact that this dessert has been known for generations in certain New England boarding schools as Fish Eyes
and Glue slow you down about trying it. It's pretty good, and
here again apples work their soothing magic. (I like it fair; my
husband says, "I always loved it, but it's funny, hardly anybody
else at school did.")

You might have some trouble finding the large pearl tapioca
that makes a true Fish Eyes and Glue. There must not be much
call for it these days, but it is stocked by some delicacy stores,
of all things. You could make an apple tapioca out of instant
tapioca (there's a recipe on the box), but this would be a sort
of Minnow Eyes and Glue and not quite the same.

2 *tablespoons pearl tapioca*	*⅓ cup sugar*
2 *cups water*	*A dash of salt*
2 *largish apples, peeled, cored*	
and cut into chunks	

Soak the tapioca in the water for at least 3 hours—12
is better. Cook over very low heat until the pearls are
transparent; 45 to 50 minutes should do it. Stir now
and then. Now combine the apples and sugar in a well-
buttered baking dish. Add the dash of salt to the tapioca and pour onto the apple mixture. Bake at 350°,
stirring 2 or 3 times, for about 1 hour, or until the apples are very tender. Cool, then chill.

This isn't actually quite the way I remember apple tapioca
from my school days. I think we had a boiled-all-the-way version,
cooked long enough so the apples just about dissolved. This way's

better, I think. If you want the other version, you might try substituting sweetened applesauce for the raw apples and sugar in this recipe.

One tricky thing: These are the amounts of pearl tapioca and water and the cooking times that work for the brand of tapioca I have. But I've seen recipes that call for half this amount of water and only 20 minutes boiling. So if the general recipes for tapioca on the package you buy call for shorter cooking times, use less water. You want the consistency to be distinctly gluelike, if you can bear the thought.

Baked Apples

Baked apples are another of the foods-to-make-you-feel-better that are remembered from the childhoods of most of us. There are as many ways to fix them as there were people (mothers, for instance) cooking in those days, but you won't find recipes for them in many books. (The assumption is that everyone is born knowing how to bake an apple.) Here's a recipe that works well.

Core the apple almost down to the bottom, but not quite. Pare off the top ⅓ to ½ of the peel. Fill the cavity with sugar, white or brown, mixed, if you like, with a dash or two of cinnamon and nutmeg or pumpkin pie spice. Add a few raisins or nuts, too, if that's what happened to the apples in your house as a child. Top with 1 teaspoon of butter.

Put in a buttered serving dish. Cover the bottom of the dish with a tablespoonful or two of water. Lay a piece of foil over the apple. Bake at 350° until tender —probably at least 45 minutes.

Serve at any temperature that appeals, plain or with a little cream. You'll feel eight years old again.

Apple Dumpling

Apples are just about number one on the nostalgia list. (And, therefore, right up there with the top soothers.) Probably *the* most nostalgic thing you can do with an apple is to turn it into a dumpling.

> For each dumpling, core and peel an apple. (You can leave the skin on—many people do—but it's apt to be tough.) Fill the cavity with white or brown sugar mixed with a dash of spice (cinnamon, nutmeg or pumpkin pie spice). Add a few raisins or nuts, if you want. Or fill the cavity with jam. Top with 1 teaspoon of butter. Enclose in a 6-inch square of unbaked pastry (page 231) or biscuit dough (page 142). Brush the top with milk. Add to the baking dish a syrup made by briefly boiling together ½ cup water, ¼ cup sugar and 1 teaspoon of butter. Bake at 400° for 45 minutes. Serve with cream.

The apple dumpling, as you can see, is just a baked apple in a cocoon. It's a nice cocoon, though.

Baked Bananas

Can you imagine making a meal of baked bananas on an evening when you don't have what it takes to cook or eat anything strenuous, but crave something nice and sumptuous? I can.

I just did it. It's every bit as good as it sounds, and was just right for tonight. *Tomorrow* I'll be good.

2 bananas	*Grated peel of ½ orange or 1*
½ lemon	*teaspoon dried orange peel*
3 to 4 tablespoons brown sugar	*2 tablespoons butter*
Cinnamon, nutmeg	*3 to 4 tablespoons rum (optional)*

Peel the bananas; cut them in half lengthwise, then crosswise. Put into a well-buttered baking dish. Squeeze the lemon juice onto the bananas, then crumble on the brown sugar. Dash on the cinnamon and nutmeg, then the orange peel. (Or substitute lemon peel. Or lime—which reminds me—lime juice is good in this instead of lemon.) Now dot with butter. If you're using the rum, sprinkle it on now or save it for after the baking; then warm it, pour it on and set fire to it. If you're having the bananas for a whole meal, omit the rum (for me, anyway). Omit the spices and citrus peel, too, if they don't appeal.

Bake at 350° for 20 to 25 minutes, basting once or twice, until the bananas look soft and beautifully glazed.

Serve with whipped cream, if you like, or hard sauce (you'll find a recipe on page 162) or, perhaps, vanilla ice cream, but those frills are absolutely unnecessary. Baked bananas don't need *anything* at all added to them.

Baked-in-the-Skin Banana

When you feel a yen for something that's hot, smooth, bland, elemental, easy and quick, this could be it (unless oatmeal better suits your mood).

Break a banana off the bunch with some care, so the skin won't be broken at all. Bake at 375° for 20 minutes. To serve, simply put on a plate; make a slit the length of the skin; eat with a fork or spoon.

A marvelous meal when you don't really want anything to eat or a good meat accompaniment or dessert.

Candied Quinces

Until very recently, it seemed impossible to find a quince in our part of the world. Suddenly, they're all over the place, at roadside stands and even supermarkets.

Have you ever encountered a quince? They look a little strange until you gently remove the natural grey fuzz they come equipped with. Then they resemble a cross between a green apple and a pear. They smell fabulous, just fabulous. Since they keep for weeks at room temperature, you can leave bowls of them around your house and everything will smell beautiful.

There seems to be a dearth of recipes for quinces, and almost all strains of this lovely fruit do have to be cooked to be palatable. One thing to know: as quinces ripen, they turn from green to yellow. After that, all you have to know is that the main secret to quince cookery is to treat them just as you would apples. For instance, you can bake them, make them into a pie or just candy them.

2 cups pared and sliced quinces
2 tablespoons butter

3 tablespoons brown sugar or 3 tablespoons granulated sugar and ¼ cup heavy cream

Gently stew the quince slices in the butter until they are soft and light brown. Stir often. Add the sugar and continue to cook and stir until the slices are glazed—candied, that is. If you use granulated sugar add the heavy cream at the same time so that it caramelizes—candies —nicely.

You can't believe how good quinces are until you try them, and they seem to share the soothing quality of apples, or perhaps I only feel that way because I like the taste so much.

This recipe is adapted from one put out by the H. A. Kaprielian Ranches, 9234 South Alta Avenue, Reedley, California 03654. I'm sure that if you write them, they'd be glad to send you more recipes and perhaps tell you where to buy quinces. Or if all else fails, plant a couple of quince trees (not the sort that only bears flowers, not fruit!) and wait a good bit for your calming candied quince.

Mary's Chocolate Sauce
For eating by the spoonful or other use

For instance, you could very well put some of this chocolate sauce on top of ice cream or cake. You don't *have* to eat it from a spoon in odd moments, but that's one of its more pleasant uses, and a fast way to grab some of chocolate's quick energy.

⅓ cup butter	*1 cup confectioner's sugar*
1½ squares (1½ ounces) unsweetened chocolate	*1 cup cream*
	2 teaspoons vanilla

Combine all the ingredients in the top of a double boiler. Cook over simmering water until the sauce is as thick as you want it to be. (It will thicken more as it cools.)

Keep refrigerated. Eat at will.

Indian Pudding

You don't have to be Indian to enjoy Indian Pudding. You don't even have to be related to any Pilgrims, though this pudding is a direct descendant of desserts served in old New England. By a tradition strong enough to be almost a rule of life in some sectors, this is what cooked all day every Saturday in a slow oven along with the baked beans.

As Indian Puddings go, this one is almost "instant," as it bakes for only an hour.

2 cups milk	1 egg, beaten
3 tablespoons cornmeal	½ teaspoon cinnamon
1 tablespoon butter	A large dash each of ginger, nutmeg and salt
½ cup dark molasses	
2 teaspoons granulated sugar	½ cup cold milk

Heat the 2 cups of milk just to the boiling point in the top half of a double boiler over direct heat. Slowly mix in the cornmeal, stirring constantly. Place over boiling water and cook for 15 minutes. Add the butter, molasses, sugar, egg and seasonings. Cook and stir until somewhat thickened.

Put into a well-buttered 1½-quart baking dish. Pour the ½ cup of cold milk on top of the mixture and bake at 350° for 1 hour. Serve hot with vanilla ice cream, whipped cream, just plain cream or even, in desperation, milk. Do as they do at Durgin-Park, a wonderful old restaurant in Boston, and serve your Indian Pudding in big soup plates. (Their strawberry shortcake is big enough for them to serve it in soup plates, too, and you should see how thick they slice their roast beef.)

Serve 2 to 4.

If you don't want to wait even one hour for Indian Pudding to bake, perhaps you'll be lucky enough to have found some in cans, all ready to go. The B&M Company puts out a good version, but I've never seen it on grocery shelves anywhere except in the inner reaches of New England.

Apple Sauce

Good old apple sauce. You'd hardly know you were eating anything, if it weren't for the delicious taste. There are some pretty good apple sauces on the market, but this is one of the times when making something yourself really pays off. The taste and texture of the homemade is quite a revelation if you've never had it before. Making it is very easy, too.

4 apples
2½ cups water

Sugar to taste—¾ cup makes it rather sweet and tastes right to me

Cut the apples into quarters without peeling them; remove the cores, seeds, stems, blossom ends and any blemishes. Combine with the water and boil slowly for 35 minutes, or until the apples have become a mush and completely left the skins. Remove the skins, add the sugar and either eat it warm right then or chill it for an hour or two.

This recipe is fairly revolutionary just because of its simplicity. Most other directions for making apple sauce call for peeling the apples first and puréeing them at some point. Some call for poaching apple slices in a syrup of sugar and water. This one evolved from a jelly-making session. The peels are left on during the cooking because they add color and flavor and because it's easier this way. And who knows? Perhaps there's some mysterious, not yet discovered vitaminlike substance in the skins that helps you feel better.

Strawberry Sherbet

As with some of the other things in this book, you can't make strawberry sherbet at the last moment; you have to know ahead of time when you are going to need to be soothed. That shouldn't be too hard. There are lots of times you have plenty of advance warning: when you're off to explain things to the Internal Revenue Service, when you're asked to come see the principal about one of your children, when you have an appointment at the dentist's, etc. At times like these, it's nice to know you have strawberry sherbet to come home to.

Strawberry sherbet isn't just soothing; it's festive and luxurious. But then, festivity and luxury can be extremely soothing, can't they? My own love for it dates back to a boarding school I went to where every May, on an occasion known as Founder's Day, we and the assembled old grads were fed lobster sandwiches and strawberry sherbet. We looked forward to it all year.

To make strawberry sherbet at any time of the year, use the frozen, sliced strawberries. Put two 10-ounce packages of them, thawed, into a blender container with the juice of 1 lemon and 2 tablespoons of sugar. Blend thoroughly, then combine with 2 stiffly beaten egg whites. (You can fold the egg whites in, or you can slowly add the strawberry purée to the beaten egg whites, running an electric mixer slowly so as not to splatter all over the kitchen.) Put into ice trays or, better, into a pan. (I have a covered enamel one, about 7 x 4 x 3 inches, that seems just right.) Cover and freeze, stirring every half hour or so to bring the more frozen edges into the center.

This recipe makes enough sherbet to take care of the emotional emergencies of you and one or two friends, or to serve as a regular dessert for five or six.

If you use fresh strawberries, treat them the same way, but add ¼ cup of sugar to 1 pint of berries, or use enough to make the purée taste sweet enough to you. And make sure the sugar is dissolved before you add the egg whites.

If you'd rather have raspberry sherbet, make it the same way, but strain the purée to remove the raspberry seeds.

Vinegar Candy

Just the *thought* of how vinegar candy smells when it's cooking makes my mouth water. It's just the power of suggestion of anything acid (they say an entire brass band can be rendered unable to play by the sight of one small child sucking on a lemon). Once this confection is cooked, though, the real bite of the vinegar is gone.

2 tablespoons butter   ½ cup vinegar
2 cups sugar

Melt the butter in a saucepan, then add the sugar and vinegar. Stir over medium heat until the sugar has dissolved. Boil gently, stirring occasionally, until the mixture reaches the stage you desire (see below). Pour into a large buttered pan.

How long to cook the mixture depends on what you want from your vinegar candy. I made it frequently throughout my childhood and, because I didn't have a candy thermometer and was a dumb cluck about things like "the soft ball stage" and the "hard crack stage," it came out in many different ways, all of them delicious.

The best, I think, is to cook the mixture to the hot side of the crack stage, about 295° to 300°. The result will be a brittle candy when it cools; you just whack it to break it up.

If you cook it less—to 275°, say—the candy will be softer and more chewy. So chewy it may pull out all your fillings. You can pull it like taffy if it's cooked to this stage.

And if you cook it more—to 325° or more, until it turns brown—you will have a nice burnt-sugar taste, somewhat like Callard and Bowswer's Treacle Brittle. And believe me, it will indeed be brittle.

A little trick: You can cook any candy that has to be boiled to a specific temperature in an electric fryer-cooker. Mix the ingredients before plugging it in. Then set the dial for the temperature you want and when the light goes out, you're there.

Snow Candy, or Sugar-on-Snow

In this world of substitutes and artificial alternatives, one fact remains unassailable: you can't make snow candy without snow. I don't know if you'd even *want* snow candy (or sugar-on-snow, another name for it) without the stimulus of watching snowflakes come down. But once you've had snow candy, and especially if you've just had the first snowfall of the season, and even more so if there's someone young around to say, "Please, may we make snow candy," you're hooked.

> Start some maple syrup simmering on the stove, say ½ cup or a little more for each person participating. Now have some new, fresh snow packed into a shallow pan and brought indoors. Test the readiness of the syrup by pouring a little on the snow: it should stay pretty much on the surface and solidify. If it sinks through the snow and dissolves, cook it down some more. When it's just right, it will turn into snow candy when it hits the snow and can be picked up and eaten in a few moments. You can pour it over the snow in strings or in globs, but just pour a little at a time. If you want creamier candy, stir the syrup around in the snow.

Obviously, the freshness of the snow is vital. Old snow equals dirty snow equals inedible candy. For several years we had a garden apartment in New York City, grime capital of the Western world. But even there we had snow candy, though we had to rush out to get our snow while it was still coming down, before the soot had a chance to take over.

Shortbread

Several of my happiest summers were spent with my grandparents at a log house they built at Mike Ament's fishing camp on Little Vermillion Lake in extreme northwestern Ontario. ("As

far North as you can go by car, then six miles more by water.")
The car trip was interesting, especially the year the party con-
sisted of two grandparents, Josie (their wonderful cook-maid-
etc.), three boy cousins, me, everyone's luggage and enough food
to last for weeks. All in one car, with a tiny open trailer bouncing
along behind. We picked up the groceries at the supermarket
nearest to our destination, which happened to be in Port Arthur,
300 miles from the camp. Each of us was allowed to lay in a
supply of our own special food, whatever we were apt to yearn
for in the north woods. Mine was shortbread. Nowadays, I make
it myself, this way.

½ pound butter (2 sticks)
½ cup sugar
2½ cups white flour

*½ cup rice flour (if you don't
have rice flour, use 2¾ cups
white flour, instead; the shortbread will be* almost *as good)*

Cream together the butter and sugar. Sift the flours
together and start to work them into the butter a little
at a time, using a wooden spoon.

When the dough is too stiff to mix with the spoon,
knead with your fingers until all of the flour is absorbed
into the mixture.

Pat firmly into a 7-x-11-inch cake pan. Prick with
a fork over the entire surface. Flute the edges with the
back of a teaspoon.

Bake for ½ hour at 250°, lower the heat to 200°
and bake for another 1½ hours, or until the shortbread is golden brown. (In my oven this takes 2 hours
at 200°, not 1½.) Cut into fingers while still warm.

This is *real* Scottish shortbread—it's from *The Highland Fling
Cookbook* (Atheneum, 1971), by Sara MacLeod Walker, a na-
tive of Scotland, who should know.

And it's every bit as good as what I used to buy. It's not every childhood memory that holds up this well. With your own home-made shortbread, though, you don't get those nice tartan tins that come with the Scottish sort. That's the only problem. Well, that and the time involved.

Madeleines

If you've read Marcel Proust's *Remembrance of Things Past,* you'll always be drawn to the thought of *madeleines.* To the narrator of that marvelous book—seven books, really—they sym-bolized his dreams of home and childhood. He dipped his in a cup of tea; you don't have to.

To make them properly, you need special French fluted *madeleine* tins. But the flavor and texture are the same if the *madeleines* are made in small muffin tins. If you're making them just for yourself, and if real *madeleines* didn't figure largely in your childhood, these will do nicely.

2 eggs at room temperature, sep-arated
½ cup sugar
½ cup flour
A dash of salt

1 teaspoon baking powder
1 teaspoon orange flower water or rum or vanilla
2 teaspoons cold plain water
¼ pound butter, melted

Combine the egg yolks, sugar, flour, salt, baking pow-der, orange flower water and plain water, in that order. Stir in the melted butter. Then fold in the egg whites, which you have beaten stiff.

Butter about 18 *madeleine* or muffin tins well, then

flour them. Fill ¾ full with the above mixture. Bake
at 425° for 10 minutes, or until the edges are brown.
Turn each *madeleine* over so the bottom side can dry.
Let them sit in a turned-off oven for 5 minutes more.
I like these sprinkled with confectioner's sugar.

The method here is simpler and quicker than in most *madeleine* recipes, but the little cakes that result taste the same as those
done in more laborious ways.

Pecan Wafers

As quick a little cookie as you could ever find to assuage a
sweet tooth. As good a one, too.

¾ cup light brown sugar   *1 cup ground pecans*
1 egg white, unbeaten

Mix the brown sugar, egg white and pecans with a
fork. Drop in little dabs onto a well-greased cookie
sheet. Bake at 300° until the edges turn light brown;
this doesn't take long, ten minutes or less, so keep an
eye on the situation. You'll have to let the cookies cool
slightly before removing them from the sheet.

You can eat these all up in as short a time as it takes to make
them. And just think—there's no flour at all in them. They're
also a good way to use up that egg white you're left looking at
after making so many other things that require thickening with
a yolk. Someone, probably Peg Bracken, has said to give these

egg whites to the cat. A fine idea, but making pecan wafers is even finer.

English Oatmeal Squares

"Cookies," said someone I know when I asked her what food did the most to soothe her. She thought a minute more, then nodded her head emphatically and said, "Yes, definitely cookies." Within two minutes she was talking about how hard it is for her to lose weight. I have the same problem, and it's gotten worse since I was introduced to these squares, the recipe for which my friend Moyra Coley brought with her when she moved from England to New Jersey and with which numerous local waistlines are being ruined.

These cookies are elemental—nothing in them but oatmeal, brown sugar and butter, if you don't count the dash of salt. They have a sort of toffee taste, and they're chewy, easy to make and quite wonderful.

¾ cup butter (1½ sticks)	2¼ cups oatmeal
¾ cup light brown sugar	A pinch of salt

Melt the butter in a saucepan. Add the brown sugar, then the oatmeal and the salt. Turn out into a square or rectangular pan, the sort you'd bake a one-layer cake in. Press the mixture down as you spread it in the pan. Bake at 350° for 25 to 30 minutes, at which point the mixture, in Moyra's words, is "soft and bubbly" but beginning to brown just a little around the edges.

Remove from the oven. Let sit for a minute or two, until the bubbling stops. Cut into squares or rectangles.

(If you put this off, the cutting will be difficult.) Let cool in pan, then remove and devour.

Moyra's recipe was all in ounces, and it called for demerara sugar and rolled oats. But she says the brown sugar's better in this. And even quick-cooking oats work out fine.

BEVERAGES

HERE ARE GROUPED TOGETHER most of the liquids that soothe, calm or cheer up different sorts of people afflicted with various moods.

I really can't suggest that you make a whole meal out of these. In tea, for instance, there's no nourishment. In the case of martinis and other alcoholic drinks, making an entire meal of them . . . well, I just can't recommend it, though there are people who do it. Many of these beverages, however (cocoa, for one), are good for times when you can't face solid food.

You'll find the whole-meal beverages in the chapter on Odds and Ends; these are eggnogs, milkshakes and two sorts of liquid "bearable breakfasts." (Even with these, though, you'd be wise to take a vitamin-mineral pill or two on the side, if you plan to substitute them for many meals.)

Cocoa

Cocoa is one of my own personal downfalls. When I'm terribly tired, too tired to sleep, this is what I crave, and I have the unfortunate habit of asking someone else to make it for me. The problem is that I only want it when I'm too exhausted to make it for myself. It's amazing anyone still lives with me.

> Make cocoa right in the mug or cup you will drink it from. Measure the milk by pouring it into the mug, then start it heating in a pan. Put 1 heaping spoonful of cocoa into the mug, then 2 heaping teaspoons of sugar. Combine these, then add just about 1 teaspoon of water and mix until the whole thing looks like chocolate frosting. (What it really looks like is mud, but that doesn't sound very appetizing.) By then the milk should be hot, just below the boiling point. Stirring the "frosting" (or mud) all the while, pour the milk slowly into the mug.

Presuming you haven't been able to persuade someone else to make the cocoa for you, hop right into bed and sip the gorgeous brew while it's hot; then close your eyes and go right off to sleep. (Don't wait too long. The heat of the cocoa and its general soothing qualities will put you to sleep, but after a while the caffeine that's in cocoa will start to work on you, and sleep won't be so easy.)

Chocolate Egg Cream

The chocolate egg cream contains neither egg nor cream. It is, however, chocolate.

It is a New York City specialty, and its strangely unapt name is merely typical of that town where very little makes sense. Many New Yorkers have acquired an addiction to this drink. One cab driver told me that he survives the daily nerve-shattering of his job only because of frequent stops for chocolate egg creams.

> If you really want one of these, put 2 or 3 large spoonfuls of chocolate syrup in a tall glass. Add an inch or so of milk. Fill the glass up with club soda; stir.

I tried one once and promptly went back to chocolate milkshakes. They're *my* addiction.

Chocolate Milkshakes, Frosteds, Cabinets— or Whatever They Call Them Where You Live

The chocolate milkshake is probably the most sustaining food of all. It can get you through anything in the world with energy to spare. It's pepping, cheering and a general boon.

I once had only fifteen minutes to get across town in New York to a job interview, and I was half-starved and feeling rather weak in the knees. I popped into a drugstore, ordered a chocolate milkshake to go, hopped into a cab, drank the shake as we bounced crosstown and arrived at the interview feeling marvelous. Got the job, too.

Somehow no one seems to realize that it's perfectly simple to make a milkshake at home in the blender.

¼ cup chocolate syrup	*1 or 2 scoops ice cream—vanilla*
1 cup milk	*or chocolate*

Just combine these ingredients and whirl in the blender. That's all! For a chocolate malted, add (guess what) . . . malt, available in most supermarkets. For even more energy and richness, add an egg. For double-chocolate flavor, use chocolate ice cream, but the usual drugstore chocolate shake is made with vanilla.

If you're heretic enough to want a milkshake of another flavor and color, just stock up on other syrups—strawberry, blueberry, etc.—and other ice creams.

About the nomenclature of those marvels: Long years ago if you asked for a chocolate *milkshake,* at least in Connecticut, where I lived then, you'd get something closely resembling chocolate milk. To have it made with ice cream you had to ask for a *frosted.* Now, though, when I ask for a *frosted,* I usually get a blank look in reply. *Cabinet* is—or, at least, was—the term in Rhode Island. At a New Jersey lunch counter I recently saw both *milkshake* and *frosted* listed on the menu. I asked the waitress what the difference was between them. The look she gave me said, "How could anyone be so dumb?" What she actually said out loud was, "The *milkshake*'s made with one scoop of ice cream; the *frosted* has two."

But whatever the name in local use, just be sure your milkshake isn't going to be of the prefabricated type that comes slowly oozing out of big silvery machines. They're so thick and synthetic that they don't do anything at all for you, or at least not for me. Maybe for you they're the very thing.

Tea

Don't forget about tea when you need something soothing. A friend of mine who had five children in five years tells me that when they were all small she would take a little time off every afternoon and say to them, "I have to have my tea for comfort now." Tea *is* comforting . . . refreshing . . . cheering . . . soothing . . . calming . . . good stuff.

When Ben Wood, a friend of my family, was head of the American end of the Tea Council, he used to send his friends, including us, some lovely Darjeeling tea every Christmas. We were sad when he changed jobs and became director of the Glass Container Association. But with the holidays came our usual tea from him, in a glass canister with this note:

"To me a cup of fine Darjeeling
Exemplifies the Christmas season.
I cannot let the custom pass
Although this year the tea's in glass."

Experiment with different sorts of tea. Aside from Darjeeling, there's smoky Lapsong Soochong, dependable Earl Grey, aromatic English Breakfast tea, perfumy Jasmine, pervasive Gunpowder and lots of others, including that orangy, spicy blend, Constant Comment.

If you don't want to make a whole potful, make your cup into a miniature teapot. Rinse it out with hot water. Put the tea leaves into some sort of straining gadget. You can find a round sort on a chain in most hardware stores, or there's a fine West German kind that has one end that's like the handle of a spoon. Or make the tea in one cup and strain it into another. Steep for three minutes. Add whatever you like in the way of lemon, milk or cream, or sugar. Ben Wood used to say that at least a drop of milk was essential to bring out the full flavor of the tea, but of course then you don't have the sparkling *look* of plain tea, and that's one of the nicest things about it to some of us.

The basic "rules" for tea-making: start with fresh, cold water;

bring it to a full boil; pour over tea leaves in a pot you've pre-heated with hot water; use one teaspoonful tea for each cup of water (and "one for the pot," if you like); brew for three to five minutes.

Tea with Rum

Tea with rum. Yum!

Just add an appropriate amount of rum (how much is up to you) to a cup of nice hot tea. Add sugar and lemon, if you want—a clove and/or a cinnamon stick if you feel that spice would be nice.

Drink enough tea with rum, and you'll absolutely feel better in body and mind, because you'll be sound asleep.

Sassafras Tea

First, find a sassafras tree or a health food store.

O.K.—now you have your sassafras. But neither the tree nor, usually, the health food store will tell you what to do with it. Here it is.

Add 4 tablespoons of sassafras chips to 2 cups of water. Boil for about 20 minutes; strain. Serve sweetened (with honey, perhaps) or not, as you prefer. The same chips can be used 2 or 3 times.

And what will sassafras tea do for you? I'm not quite sure. It's supposed to cure any number of ailments. All I know is it truly does seem to make you feel good.

Ginger Tea and Ginger Ale

When you can't face food, it's often because there's something wrong with your stomach, and ginger is the remedy of the ages for this situation. You can brew ginger tea from fresh ginger root or from the dried powder, or you can just sip a nice cold bottle of ginger ale. I don't quite go along with the company that has said in its ads that its ginger ale "tastes like love," but I must say that there are times when it tastes like the only thing you could possibly get down, and it, like the ginger tea, does have a soothing effect.

> *Fresh Ginger Tea:* Take a piece of fresh ginger root the size of a fifty-cent piece. Mince it, put it in a cup or mug and pour on boiling water. Strain if you wish, but it's not necessary. You'll like this a lot better if you add some sugar. Fresh ginger root is available in markets that cater to a Spanish or Chinese clientele, and in small cans labeled "green ginger" in fancy-food shops. To preserve, peel, put in a small jar, cover with sherry and keep in the refrigerator. (The small amount of peel on the canned green ginger doesn't have to be removed.)
>
> *Dried Ginger Tea:* Proceed as above, but just use ¼ teaspoon of the regular spice-cabinet ground ginger in your cup of boiling water. Again, sugar helps. Without it, these teas are, to put it mildly, quite startling. But with the added sugar, you'll just think you're drinking an exceptionally good, though heated, ginger ale.

As to whether to use the fresh ginger tea, ground ginger tea or a bottle of ginger ale, I'd just go by what appeals to you, and by what you have on hand.

Camomile Tea

There are still doctors in the world, and not just homeopathic practitioners, who actually prescribe camomile tea for their patients who seem in need of a soothing, refreshing tonic. Of all the herb teas, this infusion of the dried flowers of a daisylike member of the aster family is probably the oldest and most used —and it works!

Camomile is available in most health food stores and also in delicacy stores, where you'll find it in tea bags, put up by John Wagner & Sons of Ivyland, Pennsylvania, a good, reliable old spice and herb house.

> If you are using the tea bags, just steep for 3 to 5 minutes, then add sugar or honey to taste and perhaps a slice of lemon. If you can't find the bags, use the dried blossoms at the rate of 1 teaspoon of camomile to each cup of boiling water.

The resulting tea is a deep yellow and quite pretty. It tastes like summer, of meadow flowers with just a slight overtone of new mown hay.

Aside from the other benefits you should receive from camomile tea, it might be soothing just to know that, according to the Wagner company, this brew was thought by the ancient Egyptians to have powerful qualities of age prevention.

Rosemary Tea

Rosemary is for remembrance, perhaps, but rosemary tea is for calming down the nervous system and making you forget you had the jitters. It's especially good when, say, you're going to bed and want something hot but non-alcoholic, non-fattening and non-caffeine-ridden.

Make it just as you would regular tea, but use a heaping teaspoon of dried rosemary leaves or a tablespoon of fresh. Steep 3 to 5 minutes; strain. Add, if you want, a little honey and/or lemon juice.

Sleep tight.

Slippery Elm Tea

This is supposed to do wonders for the common cold. Truthfully, I have not tried it yet, but come my next cold, I plan to. It certainly couldn't do any harm, and it was relied on so much by our forefathers and mothers that it probably will help. Just taking anything so steeped in tradition is bound to make you feel better.

The directions I have come from an ancient book, *Every Day Cook Book and Family Compendium,* which features not only recipes, but such items as a cure for being struck by lightning, how to keep your lamp wicks in good shape, how to clean corsets and how to make violet ink. The slippery elm instructions do not give the amounts to use, but I assume it would go like this:

2 tablespoons slippery elm bark   *1 teaspoon lemon juice*
2 cups boiling water   *Sugar to taste (optional)*

The bark should be broken into bits. Place it in a pot or bowl, then pour on the boiling water. Let it steep until cold. Strain, reheat, add the lemon juice and, if desired, some sugar. Drink while hot—and feel better.

If you happen to be out of slippery elm, you'll find it available at many health food shops.

Barley Water

I have read somewhere that barley water is the secret of the famous English complexions. Supposedly even the ladies of the royal family use it, but whether they pat it onto the skin or drink it I can't recall. One transplanted Englishman I know drinks it, though, in a ready-made, bottled version. His American wife is kept busy trying to find it in her local stores. I have gotten the impression from her husband that he drank this brew for health and peace of mind.

Here's an old American way to make your own barley water.

Boil 5 tablespoons of pearl barley (the grain, not the noodle) in 1 cup water for 5 minutes. Add 4 more cups of water and continue to boil until the liquid is reduced by half; strain. Sweeten to taste with granulated sugar.

Flavor with sliced lemon or nutmeg, or so says a nineteenth-century cookbook. You might like the barley water better if you added lemon or lime juice. That way, thoroughly chilled, it tastes surprisingly good, and perhaps it's just the power of suggestion, but it really does seem to have a soothing effect.

Cambric Tea

I'm not quite sure what was in the cambric tea a childhood friend's governess used to give us, but it seemed exciting and grown-up to be having a tea party of our own. Probably our cups and our little teapot contained well-sugared hot milk with a teaspoon or two of tea for flavor, color and glamour.

Cambric tea is not one of my more devastating suggestions, so I won't devote much time or space to it. It's just a thought. Perhaps it will kindle a memory for someone or fill a need, since it is so simple and undemanding. I think I'll try it myself the next time I can't face food, and I think I feel one of those times coming on right now. . . .

Champagne

When you're down, when you're sad, when your life seems to be a mess, when you feel absolutely seedy—treat yourself to a split of champagne. It will probably cost less than going to a new movie, and it will do more for you than a trip to a psychiatrist.

Whiskey Sours

If you have to somehow get through a few days of stress, you might try putting part—but only part—of your reliance on a whiskey sour or two before lunch and/or dinner. They seem to have remarkable endurance-inducing properties, especially if they are made sweeter than usual. They've come in handy, for instance, when a certain mother was trying to get things ready for her daughter's wedding and the daughter was working and only available for planning and dashing about at lunchtimes and on Saturdays. Both mother and daughter say they could never have gotten everything done and survived the whole thing without the whiskey sours–sweet with which they began their lunches during that period.

3 ounces whiskey—rye, bourbon,   2 tablespoons lemon juice
Scotch or anything you like   3 tablespoons sugar

Shake whiskey, lemon juice and sugar together with ice; strain into two stemmed glasses, or save half for a refill (or cut the recipe in half).

For whiskey sours on the rocks, just pour half of this mixture over lots of ice cubes (some of them cracked) in an old-fashioned glass.

Remember these, too, when you are more or less compelled to have a drink at lunch but want to be able to get a lot of work done in the afternoon. One or even two whiskey sours never yet sank anyone into anything resembling the stupor that lunchtime martinis can bring on.

Brandy Milk Punch

A few years after World War II, my family and I met a young man named David McGregor. We struck up a friendship that was in some ways quite a symbiotic relationship: David had some beautiful old cognac he had acquired while serving with the Quartermaster Corps in France; we had a Jersey cow. For a long time, every Sunday after church, David, bottle in hand, would arrive at our house. We'd combine some of his brandy with some of that incomparably creamy milk, add a little sugar and have a calm, delightful interlude before lunch.

I'll leave the proportions up to you. One and a half ounces of brandy, maybe, to about a cup of milk (if you don't have a Jersey cow, you might substitute cream for part of the milk) and a little sugar—start with a teaspoon and keep tasting until it seems right to you. (If you keep the tasting up long enough, you could reach a point where you don't much care about *how* sweet it is, or about much of anything else, either.)

Shake with ice or pour over ice cubes in old-fashioned glasses. Sprinkle nutmeg on top if you don't feel it destroys the taste of the brandy.

Lager and Lime

My son, Bob, went to Scotland last summer. He brought back a Shetland sweater for his older sister and one for me, a tweed suit for himself and a tremendous liking for a drink he discovered over there: lager and lime. To make it, you put an ounce or so of Rose's lime juice into a glass or beer mug and add a bottle of light beer.

Does that mean an end to innocence, to his eggnog days? Not at all. He now has eggnog at least once during the day and lager and lime at least once during the evening, and he is always now the calmest, most soothed person you ever saw.

Claret Lemonade and Sangria

At a boarding school I went to, there were a number of privileges connected with being a senior. Things such as being allowed to sleep all the way to nine-thirty on Saturday mornings and being excused from certain study halls.

One of the best privileges was the annual senior trip to a performance of the Boston Pops. Oh, the glamour of it! And the incredible fact that for that one evening out of all our time at school, we were allowed to have an alcoholic beverage—Claret Lemonade. (Even at the Boston Pops, the school's vehement rule against smoking was enforced; but at one of these concerts, the air was so thick with the cigarette smoke of others that the headmistress turned to us and said, "Well, girls, I can't stop you from breathing, at any rate.")

> To make Claret Lemonade in quantity, half-fill a pitcher with ice cubes. Onto this pour a bottle of claret —red Bordeaux wine—then the juice of 3 lemons, 4 or 5 slices of orange and enough simple syrup (equal amounts of sugar and water boiled together, then cooled) to make the lemonade as sweet as you'd like. (Start with ¼ cup, then add more to taste.) Let it sit for about a half hour to mellow. Serve over ice in tall glasses or goblets.

The resemblance to *sangria* is clear, but Claret Lemonade seems to be indigenous to North America, while *sangria* made its happy appearance here fairly recently. (And Claret Lemonade is pretty much forgotten.)

> For *sangria,* you could just add a large squirt of club soda to the pitcher of Claret Lemonade.
> Or you could add other juice or fruit—orange, lime or pineapple juice, for instance, or pieces of peach or pear or apricot. (A tip: you can add some prepared baby-food fruit purée, especially apricot, to good effect.)

There are people who "spike" *sangria* by adding to it more potent liquids—brandy, tequila or an orange-flavored liqueur, in particular. This, to me, isn't at all necessary, or even desirable. *Sangria* should stay as innocent as Claret Lemonade; in fact, that squirt of club soda makes it even *more* innocent.

Home Remedy

My friend Anne Simons told me of this wonder-worker years ago, and it's been a standby for my family ever since, for incipient colds, flu and all that sort of nuisance. For the adults, anyway. My daughter Katie swears that it's included in some of her earliest memories, but she's absolutely wrong. What I used to make her sip when she was sick was a simple combination of lemon juice and honey. This home remedy is another matter entirely.

> Combine in a saucepan the juice of 1 lemon, about ½ cup of water and enough honey to make the mixture taste good. (For a clue, start off with 2 tablespoons.) Bring this to a boil, stirring to dissolve the honey. Pour into a mug, then add whiskey; bourbon is my choice, but surely rye, Scotch, etc., would have the same effect. Drink while it's very hot.

The amount of whiskey to add is up to you. I don't really measure: my system is to use enough water to fill a mug about three-quarters full (using the mug as a measure), add it to the honey and lemon, boil it, pour it back into the mug and then fill up the mug with bourbon.

But I forgot the most important thing. Be completely ready for bed when you make this, then hop under the covers and *stay there* while you drink the brew and afterward. You'll get very warm: you'll sweat, perspire, glow or do whatever you do along that line, and you'll yearn to throw back the covers. Be strong, though, and don't. You'll go off to sleep soon and in the morning, if you're like me, you'll wake up feeling remarkably better.

Bourbon and Honey

I think the only place I've ever drunk bourbon and honey is in bed. It's for times when I feel I'm coming down with something and one or another of the kindly people I live with says, "Why don't you just have dinner in bed?" They usually don't get much argument from me. I make myself a glassful of bourbon and honey and take it up with me, and someone brings me the wicker bedtray (an extravagance I recommend to everyone) and eventually dinner. I *always* feel better afterwards.

> *1 jigger bourbon*
> *1 tablespoon honey*

Mix together thoroughly enough to dissolve the honey
in an old-fashioned glass. Add ice.

Bourbon and honey fixed this way is especially good if you have a sore throat. The honey soothes physically, and the ice anaesthetizes. Oh, all right, the bourbon does a little anaesthetizing, too. However it works, it does help, and the pampering inherent in the whole situation doesn't hurt a bit, either.

Hot Buttered Rum

Perhaps the most pleasant way to recover from a session in the freezing cold out-of-doors is to take some anti-freeze. For hot buttered rum, one of the standard winterizers:

Heat a mug by filling it with hot water. Pour the water out, then put 1 teaspoon of confectioner's sugar in the mug with a little boiling water. Stir until the sugar dissolves, then add 1½ ounces of rum (or 2 ounces if your need of thawing is great) and a small piece, 1 teaspoon or less, of butter. Fill the mug up with boiling water.

There's another way to make hot buttered rum that I like even better. There's one simple difference in the recipes: you use hot cider instead of boiling water. You can, if you wish, sprinkle some nutmeg and/or cinnamon on top. My grandfather, a life-long teetotaler (I've been told he single-handedly kept Henry County, Iowa, dry for years), used to like to have me make this for him—without the rum, of course—when I was a teen-ager. While everybody else was fussing about how much ver-mouth to put in the martinis, he and I could discuss just how much nutmeg to use and whether or not it might be better to float the butter on top instead of putting it at the bottom of the mug first.

Sombreros

To my great delight, a son-in-law has recently come into my life. Among Craig's great contributions to our family has been one of the most soothing drinks ever, the Sombrero. Here is how he says to make it.

> *1 part Kahlúa*
> *1 part heavy cream*

Shake with ice; strain into a cocktail glass.

Definitely an after-dinner drink, at least for me. After a couple of these, I smile happily all the way up to my bed. Craig says to add that if someone is feeling fancy, a little nutmeg could be sprinkled on top of the drink.

Martinis on the Rocks

Can there be any doubt that martinis are soothing? Yes. They seem to make some people downright quarrelsome. The late Dr. Virgil Damon once wrote his ten (or was it twenty?) rules for a happy marriage. The first rule was, "Never drink martinis." And the last rule? "Never drink martinis."

Can anyone deny, though, that martinis can make your cares —if not you, yourself—fade off into utter oblivion?

My nonmeasuring, haphazard approach:

> Pour into a double old-fashioned glass the amount of gin that looks good to you. (If you'd rather measure, try 1½ ounces.) Now add 3 or 4 drops of dry vermouth. Your hand won't be steady enough (even before sampling the martini) to really confine the vermouth to 3 or 4 drops, but at least you'll have a very dry martini.
>
> Ice comes next—lots and lots of it, until the entire

glass is full of drink and ice. You may have to smash a few of the ice cubes to make this work out.

And now for me, a large twist of lemon peel. I cut off a good-sized piece of just the yellow part and twist it right over the glass. Then I rub the peel around the inside of the rim of the glass before dropping it into the drink. You, of course, may add an olive or a few little pickled onions if you'd rather.

If you prefer to have your martini "straight up" as opposed to "on-the-rocks," just chill a stemmed glass first and stir the martini very, very thoroughly with ice before pouring it into the glass. Coldness is the main trick to making a really good martini.

And the main trick to being a really good martini-drinker? Don't have more than two.

ODDS AND ENDS

HERE ARE THE UNCLASSIFIABLE ITEMS—all of them too good to omit, none of them quite fitting any other category.

Some of them are very much mood foods—just think about roasted chestnuts. Butter's here, though, because it goes with almost everything.

Some of these odds and ends could have been sneaked in with the breads—milk toast, bread and gravy and stewed crackers come to mind—but since they're so transformed, it doesn't seem right.

You'll find here eggnogs and two sorts of liquid "bearable breakfasts." Though these are fluid, they're not really beverages; they're meals, at least to me.

Fried apples belong here rather than with desserts because when they're not acting as a full meal to calm an upset psyche, they're usually served as an adjunct to meats.

Cereals are here, too, and calf's foot jelly, that super-soother of the past. And beef marrow with buttered toast, which can take care of many sorts of moods. And yogurt, that beautiful food.

So please don't pass over this chapter too quickly. It may be called "Odds and Ends," but most of the things aren't really so very odd.

Butter

Butter turns up over and over in the recipes I write (you may have noticed). This doesn't mean that I don't think you should use margarine. It can be quite good, and I use it myself fairly often in baking.

It also doesn't mean that I think you should use sweet butter. I feel I should mention this, since in one cookbook I read recently, the author said to use sweet butter in any recipe of hers or anyone else's unless the salted variety is specified. No! Sweet butter can be beautiful. It can indeed be "sweet," but most of the time it is distinctly sour. It spoils, and most of it that you buy has already turned. The sourness it acquires is not the pleasant tang of commercial sour cream; it is the unpleasant taste of cream-gone-wrong.

If you want to use sweet butter, make your own. It's not hard at all, and it's delightful. Here are some ways:

Probably the easiest way is to make butter in a blender. Put 1 cup of heavy cream in the blender container and whir it briefly. It will become first whipped cream, then butter. To help it along you can add about ½ cup of ice water after you reach the whipped cream stage. You don't have to, though, if you have a good, strong blender. Whichever way, put the resulting butter in a strainer and rinse it well under cold water. This makes about ½ cup (¼ pound) of butter.

Another easy way is one I learned from my daughter Candy when she was four. She was taught how at nursery school. Simply put heavy cream in a screw-top jar and shake it. Don't fill the jar more than half-way full; you want a lot of action. This works amazingly well. Again, rinse the butter in cold water to get rid of the milk that remains, since this seems to be what goes sour and gives that horrid taste.

Another way, but more time-consuming, is to make butter by beating heavy cream in an electric mixer. My mother discovered this one during World War II when butter was rationed, but heavy cream, I believe, wasn't. You just beat and beat and beat.

And then there's the churn, to be used only if you have a *lot* of cream (if you have a cow, in fact) or if you have a very determined urge to get back to "the old ways." You will also need a very determined arm. (Using an electric churn would be cheating.)

By any of these methods, you end up with *real* sweet butter, worth going into rhapsodies over.

To keep butter from burning when you're cooking with it at high heat, you may want to clarify it: cook it slowly over very low heat until it looks completely clear except for some sediment on the bottom of the pan. Cool a little, then strain. But cooking with half butter, half vegetable oil will accomplish the same thing.

Bananas Baked with Bacon

These make a good vegetable or main dish or even a whole meal for odd moments. And they're very soothing if, like Tit Willow, you're having trouble with your little insides.

2 bananas
Wheat germ (or dry bread crumbs,
   if need be)
Salt
Pepper

Paprika
Juice of ½ lemon
3 slices bacon, cut in half and
   briefly precooked

Slice the bananas thinly on the diagonal, so you get longish pieces. Cover the bottom of a buttered baking dish with a layer of wheat germ (or bread crumbs); use about ¼ cup. Cover with a layer of banana slices. Sprinkle lightly with salt, pepper and paprika and sprinkle on a little lemon juice. Repeat twice, if the ingredients hold out, ending with a layer of bananas sprinkled with seasonings. On top of this, lay the bacon slices. (Precook them just enough to make the fat begin to become transparent.)

Bake at 350° for about 35 minutes, or until the bacon is crisp.

Serves 1 as an entrée; 2 or 3 as a side dish.

Canadian bacon should be a good alternative to the regular sort, but in that case, you'd better dot the top layer of bananas with about 1 tablespoon of butter before baking.

Fried Mush

Could anything sound less appetizing than "fried mush"? Only if you haven't tried it. If you have, your eyes will light up at the mention of the name; I *almost* guarantee. Of course, if you're new to Fried Mush, you won't have memories of a wonderful grandmother making it. Here's what mine used to do:

> Make Cream of Wheat, following the package directions, the day before you want your Fried Mush. Put it into a buttered loaf pan and chill it. When it's cold and you're ready to eat, cut the mush into thin slices. Fry in hot fat of some sort (bacon or sausage fat, lard or butter), turning until both sides are brown. Serve with butter and maple syrup.

The slices will be crusty on the outside, soft on the inside; warm, bland and comforting. Some mush-makers use cornmeal mush; others start with hominy grits. Fine, I'm sure, and maybe I'll try them someday.

Scottish Scotch Oatmeal

The friend who told me about this particular soothing food was raised by his Scottish grandmother. This no doubt explains his love for oatmeal, but I doubt if his grandmother ever put Scotch whiskey onto Alan's porridge when he was a little boy.

Cooked oatmeal, enough for a big   1 *tablespoon honey*
   bowlful   1 *teaspoon Scotch whiskey*
1 *tablespoon butter*

Make the oatmeal in your own fashion, following the instructions on the box for either regular, quick-cooking or even instant oatmeal—or better yet, real Scottish or Irish oatmeal. Put in a bowl, top with butter, which will melt, then drizzle on the honey and Scotch.

I myself am more apt to top my oatmeal with just butter and black pepper, but then, I don't like Scotch. But even the regular sort, with milk and sugar, can do nice things for you.

Roasted Chestnuts

When I asked our friend Georganne Ross what she considered a cheering, soothing food she thought for a moment or two, then smiled and said, "roasted chestnuts." This was nice to hear, since we had just finished spending a leisurely afternoon before our fireplace, drinking tea and roasting chestnuts. Georganne had never had them before and seemed to find it a nice experience. All the rest of us did, too.

If you have one of the special chestnut pans—they resemble a long-handled frying pan with holes in the bottom—you're in luck. But if you don't, you can just wrap the chestnuts in foil. Whichever way, slit the shells of the chestnuts first. If you're cooking them in the pan, keep it moving over the fire until the chestnuts look just slightly charred. If in the foil, leave the packet over the fire for 20 minutes.

If you live in New York City, you know that one of the major winter sights there is the chestnut vendors all over town. You can smell the chestnuts, slightly acrid, definitely nostalgic, almost wherever you go. You buy them because they're good, because New York winters wouldn't be the same without them and because they help keep your hands warm.

Yogurt of Various Sorts

Viola Branch, an old friend, is the one who said, "I want yogurt when I just don't want *anything* else."

But your first taste of yogurt, if you're still at that stage, can be startling—most particularly if you start with the plain, unflavored sort, or if you try one of the brands that haven't yet quite perfected their product, or if it's over-age yogurt.

Dannon and Columbo make lovely flavored yogurts. But I'm indebted to my friend Dorothy Parker for some of the good things to do with plain yogurt she has detailed in her fascinating book, *The Wonderful World of Yogurt* (Hawthorn, 1972). I already knew that you could add various sorts of jam (blackberry-apple preserves or ginger marmalade, for instance) and come up with delicious yogurt, but Dorothy suggests some other good ideas for turning plain yogurt into something special. She also details how to make your own yogurt without a special machine. Here are some of her ideas.

> *Add fruit*—a sliced-up banana, some apple sauce, a leftover bit of cranberry sauce, cut-up figs or dates or any fresh, canned or dried fruits, with or without a little sugar. (Or with honey, my own favorite sweetener for yogurt.)
>
> *Add fresh, raw vegetables*—cut-up radishes, leaves of endive or lettuce, raw carrot or beet shavings.
>
> *Add anything left over from another meal*—herbed rice, asparagus tips in butter, artichoke hearts, cooked

yellow squash or whatever else you find tucked away in your refrigerator.

A bit of night-before-last's curry would be senational, a spoon-full of chili would be exciting, and so on. Dorothy Parker says, "One of the best surprises for me occurred when I found less than a serving of Eggplant Parmigiana and stirred *that* into my lunch-time yogurt. Ambrosia!"

If you want a yogurt soup, simply add liquid—milk, broth or whatever you have—to the plain yogurt and whatever other ingredients you have on hand.

Eggnog

Ah, eggnog! For breakfast, lunch, supper, bedtime and any time in-between. When you're tired, discouraged, depressed, up-set, jaded, nervous or any combination of these horrible states, an eggnog should fix you right up.

1 egg	*2 tablespoons sugar*
1 cup milk	*1 teaspoon vanilla*

Put everything into a blender container and buzz briefly, just long enough to make it all thoroughly ho-mogeneous. (If there are streaks of uncombined egg running through your eggnog, you won't find it sooth-ing at all.) Pour into a glass and sprinkle a little nut-meg on the top. For extra energy, use two eggs.

Try this when someone (you yourself, perhaps) says "no" to food. Almost anyone, under any circumstances, will make an exception for eggnog.

Honey-Orange Bearable Breakfast

When there's just no way you can face breakfast or at any other time you feel you really should eat *something,* you can probably manage to look this drink square in the eye and drink it down. It's smooth and it tastes delicious. It's even fairly good for you, and no problem at all to make. A sort of golden eggnog.

1 cup orange juice
1 to 3 tablespoons honey (to taste)

1 or 2 eggs (2 makes a more nourishing drink, but thicker— you'd better start with one)

Run together in the blender, pour and drink.

There; that wasn't hard at all, was it?

Coffee Bearable Breakfast

For those who find breakfast an unclimbable mountain and who also like things like coffee with cream and sugar or coffee ice cream. Black-coffee people better not try it.

1 cup milk
1 teaspoon instant coffee

2 teaspoons sugar (or to taste)
1 egg

Whirl in the blender until it's frothy. (Add a little coffee ice cream if you want this extra rich.)

Arthur Murray, he of the dancing school chain, was, as far as I know, the originator of this speedy breakfast. Because the Murrays' twin daughters were close friends of mine, I used to spend a lot of time with that delightful family. Mrs. Murray, Kathryn, is a good cook, who used to make blintzes from scratch and get up at six in the morning to make brownies. But as far as I saw, the only breakfast she was ever able to get her husband to eat was this one. A highly organized man, he couldn't see wasting time on the usual sit-down sort of thing.

Pâte Brisée and Flaky Pie Crust

Pie crust—*good* pie crust—isn't easy for some of us to make, but it's rather essential for a repertoire of mood-soothing foods. The solution for me came when I discovered *pâte brisée,* the French version. To me, it's not only better than most American pie crusts, it's also far easier.

The first *pâte brisée,* and the best, came into my personal repertoire some ten years ago via *Economy Gastronomy* by Sylvia Vaughn Thompson (Atheneum, 1963), a book that changed some of my attitudes toward cooking and made me take greater pains in certain areas, and less in others. (It also made me want Atheneum for my own publisher.)

To make enough for a one-crust pie, Mrs. Thompson says to use:

1 cup sifted flour
1 egg yolk
1 scant tablespoon sugar

1 stick (four ounces) butter, well softened (Mrs. Thompson says "vegetable butter")
1 tablespoon ice water

"Sift the flour onto the bread board, make a well in the center. Drop in the yolk and sugar, then the butter. Work the egg, sugar and butter together with your finger tips—avoiding the flour as much as possible—until a thick smooth paste has formed; now quickly blend in the surrounding flour until you have a crumbly mass that almost holds together. Work it as little as possible. Sprinkle over this the ice water, then very lightly blend it into the paste. When it will all stay—a matter of moments—pat into a flat cake, wrap in waxed paper, and set in the refrigerator for an hour." For a two-crust pie, double the ingredients.

Mrs. Thompson gives another pie crust, which she calls "My Best Flaky Pastry," and which she recommends for non-sweet use. It's good, too, and perhaps you'll feel more comfortable with it. This crust, enough for a one-crust pie, is made with:

1⅔ cups sifted flour
10 tablespoons chilled lard or butter or margarine—or a combination (Mrs. Thompson says
to use half lard, half margarine)
A dash of salt
2 to 4 tablespoons ice water

"Combine flour and 5 tablespoons lard with pastry blender or finger tips on a bread board until the texture of coarse meal; flake in the vegetable butter [or whatever] and mix until the texture of tiny peas. Add salt. Now sprinkle, a spoonful at a time, as little ice water as possible into the mixture, never hitting the same place twice. As you do this, press the moistened flour together with a fork, and whatever adheres, take out and place on a square of waxed paper, and refrigerate for an hour or more (overnight tenderizes it most)."

Now those are what I call good, clear directions, and they work most admirably. Making this crust or the *pâte brisée* may sound complicated, but believe me, they're a breeze compared to trying to figure out most directions, if you're a crust-klutz like me. And they're the two best crusts possible.

Beef Marrow Sublime

All beef marrow is superb, even if it's only the dab you suck out of a soup bone in the kitchen after making stock. But *planned* beef marrow is sublime, a Lucullan treat that just doesn't happen to be expensive. The Italians have the right attitude; they make a ritual out of it and even have a special utensil for scooping marrow out of the bones.

> Use marrow bones cut into about 2-inch lengths. Lay them flat in a roasting pan, so they rest on bone, not marrow. Bake at 350° for approximately 1 hour, or until a poke with a fork goes into the marrow easily.
> Put the bones on a large, warm plate. Provide freshly made toast, buttered or not. (I like *everything* buttered, so . . .) Scoop out a little marrow. A small-bowled iced tea or demitasse spoon will work best, unless you have one of the special Italian marrow scooper-outers. Put the marrow on a small piece of toast. On this, a few grinds from a pepper mill *and* a salt mill, if you have one. Eat.

Continue in this fashion, slowly and contentedly, until all the marrow is gone—and, possibly, all your cares as well.

Chocolate Butter

I only had chocolate butter once in my childhood, but I've certainly never forgotten it. My godfather, Bud Gibson, made it one night at our house. I heard all the grownups laughing and exclaiming down in our kitchen and wished I could be down there joining in on the fun. And then I was brought some of what they were carrying on about: chocolate butter on an English muffin! English muffins are always good, but with chocolate butter they are bliss. Years and years later I worked out how to do it:

| 1 tablespoon cocoa | A very few drops of milk or water |
| 2 tablespoons sugar | 2 tablespoons soft butter |

Combine the cocoa and sugar, then add the liquid drop by drop until you have a very thick mixture. (Just like making cocoa, page 204. In fact, this should properly be called cocoa butter, but that's something else entirely.)

Stir this mixture into the soft butter. Split and toast an English muffin and spoon on the chocolate butter. Eat right away.

This much chocolate butter will amply take care of 2 muffin halves.

Bud Gibson contributed another culinary curiosity to our house: French fried eggs. (Fry an egg quickly in deep fat instead of slowly in shallow.) These are good, and they're fun (they bubble up in a spectacular way), but they're not especially soothing.

Bud came by his innovative qualities naturally. His uncle was Charles Dana Gibson, who will probably go down in history less for his paintings and drawings and the "Gibson girl" than for the remarkable idea he had of replacing the olive in a martini with a pickled onion.

Calf's Foot Jelly

Do you remember how in old books, whenever anyone was sick, even if only with an attack of the "vapours," some kindly neighbor would bring over some calf's foot jelly? An attack of the vapours sounds rather nice; I think I'll schedule one for as soon as I finish writing this book. If a kindly neighbor wants to make me feel better, here's how to make the grand champion literary restorative:

> Simmer 4 pounds of nicely cleaned calves' feet in 4 quarts of water until the liquid is reduced to 2 quarts. Strain and let it stand overnight. Then remove all the fat and sediment and add to the remaining liquid 1 pint of wine, 3 cinnamon sticks, 4 egg whites, 1 pound of sugar and the juice and peel of 3 lemons. Boil for 10 minutes. Strain and chill until set.

The gist of this recipe comes from *Miss Beecher's Housekeeper and Healthkeeper,* a helpful book published in 1873. It does sound good, and if I can talk my butcher into getting me some calves' feet, I think I'll try it myself. As you can see, this is a sort of gelatine, an aspic, rather than the sort of jelly you put on your breakfast toast. The year 1873 must have been about the time this sort of thing went out of style, because Miss Beecher says, "The American gelatine, now very common, makes a good jelly, with far less trouble."

Crackers and Milk

The simple combination of crackers and milk is my father's idea of what to eat when he doesn't feel like having a real meal.

All my life I've watched in amazement as he happily consumed about a quart of milk and a box of saltines at one sitting. It has always seemed to cheer him up immensely. I've never tried it and doubt if I ever will, because I'm not very fond of milk. My idea of crackers and milk is Stewed Crackers, which follows—it doesn't taste as milky. But if you like plain milk and you like saltines, you're probably going to love making a whole meal of the combination.

Stewed Crackers

Milk toast's first cousin once removed, but better for those who had too much milk toast in their childhood and can't face it again.

6 single saltines	⅔ cup milk
½ cup boiling water	Salt and pepper
1 tablespoon butter	

Arrange the saltines, whole or broken up, in a single layer in a skillet or any pan big enough to hold them. Pour on the boiling water; cover. Allow to steep for a few minutes. Meanwhile, brown the butter slightly, just to a light tan, in another pan. Add the milk, salt and pepper. When this mixture's piping hot, pour it over the saltines; then pour everything into a soup plate or bowl.

If you close your eyes, especially if you have broken up the saltines, you may think you're eating oyster stew. Serves one not-too-hungry person.

Bread and Gravy

Bread and gravy, though you might not think it, is a food of rebellion. Here are just a couple of the thoughts that might go through the head of a person who sneaks the gravy out of the refrigerator, heats it up, puts it over bread and skulks away to eat it in some hidden place:

> "This is fattening food . . . well, I just don't care! I'll bet somebody wants this gravy so they can make something else out of it. That's just too bad!"

Everyone has his own points of rebellion. (Children don't usually realize it, but their parents are often *seething* with rebellion.) And everyone needs solitude at times. Bread and gravy by yourself (as opposed to the group-eating situation in which the gravy probably first appeared) accentuates your aloneness, especially if you really do sneak off somewhere to eat it. (If there's no place else you can hide, try the bathroom.)

If there's no leftover gravy around, you can buy frozen pouches of gravy with beef or gravy with turkey that are almost the same. Just follow the heating directions and serve over plain, untoasted bread.

Milk Toast

There was milk toast in my childhood; wasn't there in yours? I was a little suspicious of it at first because at that age I didn't like milk and because it didn't look at all the way I thought food *should* look. But it turned out to be pretty good, milk or no, and of course it was only given to me when the thought of real food was repellent anyway. It's not very hard to make.

Heat 1 cup of milk to which you've added a dash of salt. Meanwhile, make 1 piece of toast and spread it with butter. Put the toast into a soup bowl and pour the hot milk over it.

There are, I hear, people who add sugar to their milk toast. It's probably good that way, too.

Fried Apples

The other day I was vilely, horrendously ill. Miserable with, I guess, a "stomach bug." That day, no food. No chance. The next day, food still didn't have much appeal, but I finally thought of one thing that sounded good to me: fried apples. Fortunately, I had already figured out how to make them so they tasted the way my grandmother's used to. I have a lot of her recipes, but fried apples just aren't the sort of thing you write down. You are supposed to *know* how to cook them. Not me—and though I don't think this is quite the way I remember seeing my grandmother make them (I think she just cored the apples, sliced them, sprinkled them with sugar and fried them), these taste the closest to hers of any I've tried.

3 tasty apples	*⅓ cup sugar*
3 tablespoons bacon fat	*A dash of salt*
¼ cup water	

Quarter the apples and remove the cores; then slice them about ⅓ inch thick. Heat the bacon fat in a large, heavy (preferably iron, to be authentic) skillet. When it's fairly hot, add the apple slices and spread them out into one layer. Cover and cook over medium heat until the bottoms of the slices are slightly brown. (You have to be careful all through this operation, otherwise so easy, that the apples don't burn.) Turn the apples over with a pancake turner, cover again and cook until that side is brown. Then add the water, sugar and salt and cook the whole thing gently, uncovered, until it's all glazed and gorgeous and the syrup has just about disappeared.

Serves 1 to 3.

I hope they do as well for you in a moment of need as they did for me.

MOOD INDEX

WHEN YOU'RE COMING DOWN WITH OR
   RECOVERING FROM SOMETHING

WHEN YOU NEED QUICK STRENGTH/
   ENERGY

WHEN YOU COULD FACE BREAKFAST IF
   IT WERE SOMETHING INTERESTING

FOOD INDEX

Glenn Andrews

Glenn Andrews, a Sarah Lawrence graduate, has been an editor at Seventeen *magazine and letters correspondent for Time, Inc. For nine years she has written a column on horse racing for the* National Star Chronicle, *and has been a producer of network radio programs. Her previous book,* Impromptu Cooking, *was a selection of the Cookbook Guild. Mrs. Andrews now lives in Boca Raton, Florida, where she and her family play tennis and cook foods for various moods.*